ALSO BY CHRIS BRADY

Rascal

PAiLS

A Month of Italy

Launching a Leadership Revolution (with Orrin Woodward)

Leadership Lessons from the Age of Fighting Sail

Financial Fitness (with Orrin Woodward)

the Bitcoin Bride

a RASCAL MONEY story

CHRIS BRADY

First Edition, October 2021
10 9 8 7 6 5 4 3 2 1

Published by:
Obstaclés Press, Inc.
200 Commonwealth Court
Cary, NC 27511

ISBN: 978-0-9990440-9-4

Cover design by Christine Brady

Printed in the United States of America

for Marshall

"We are witnessing the Great Monetary Inflation – an unprecedented expansion of every form of money unlike anything the developed world has ever seen."

– *Paul Tudor Jones*

"I don't believe we shall ever have a good money again before we take the thing out of the hands of government, that is, we can't take it violently out of the hands of government, all we can do is by some sly roundabout way introduce something that they can't stop."

– *spoken by economist Friedrich Hayek in the year 1984*

1

It began with a woman.

Marcus spotted her across the proverbial crowded room, except it was outdoors at a church gathering just off campus on a perfect late summer Friday evening in Shadyside. He was already in a good mood, but now he was transfixed, like the lead in a romantic comedy when he first sees *her*.

Wearing a cobalt blue summer dress and standing in a tight little circle of friends, she was smiling, and then laughing, then shaking her head. As she did so, Marcus noticed every detail of her dark, satiny hair as it bounced and twisted just off her shoulders. He admired her slight dimples and large dark eyes. He had long since stopped listening to whatever was being said to him by his friends and was now just staring directly at her from a distance.

Nothing like this had ever happened to him.

Before that night, Marcus would have never admitted to such a thing as love at first sight. He'd dated off and on through the years and had some meaningful relationships. But love? Instant love? Nothing of the kind. He'd certainly never been so taken by the mere image of a stranger. What was happening to him, he wondered?

"It's Cassandra, with all the a's pronounced the same," she told him in their first few moments once he'd finally worked up the nerve to walk over and initiate a conversation. "Federici," she added.

"Marcus Coleman," he answered as if in a trance, noticing and immediately loving her slight Italian accent. This was followed by an awkward pause as Marcus strained for something clever to say. But Cassandra was quicker on the draw and immediately put him at ease with a little chuckle, saying, "Nice to meet you, Marcus Coleman. But I actually know who you are. You taught one of the lectures in Intro to Comp Sci back in the Spring." This was one of the larger undergraduate courses with an attendance of over a hundred students, and Marcus, as a graduate student, had been given the lecture duties for one section.

"Oh, you were in that class? I hope it made sense."

"It did! We all thought you were great," she answered. "Pointers and stacked arrays are much clearer to me now."

"Well, thanks, and good."

"There's a bench over there," she said as she motioned. "Wanna have a seat?"

"Sure," Marcus replied, amazed at his good fortune so far, and nodding a sheepish grin at Cassandra's friends as the two of them left the group.

"What year are you?" he asked, once they'd gotten situated on a dark green park bench under a Japanese maple. They had a view of the sprawling church campus, featuring a large white tent set up in the lawn area for this event—an open house for the local college students.

"I'm a junior in the fine arts school, actually. That computer class was just a lark. I was auditing it." She tucked her hair behind her ear and while doing so, a dangling earring flickered reflected sunlight. Marcus was noticing everything as if in slow motion.

"Oh. Can't be too many students from the fine arts school coming over to the engineering side," he said.

"Nope. Not too many. But that's why I like Carnegie Mellon, or one of the reasons. I can be my usual artsy self, but still feed my inner geek."

"OK, now I'm speechless. Are you for real, or am I dreaming this?" Marcus placed his hand over his heart for dramatic effect.

"That's sweet. But seriously, I've always been interested in technology, although music and the stage are my passions."

"What's your major?"

"Music composition."

"You're a songwriter?" Marcus asked.

"I wanna be."

At this point Marcus realized the shiny earrings he had noticed before were shaped like treble clefs.

"Have you written anything I could hear?"

"Maybe someday," she smiled. "But what about you? I know you're a teaching assistant for computer science, but what else?"

"I'm finishing a master's in computer engineering, and I'd begun some work toward a PhD, which is how they ended up having me help out with that class. But I'm actually thinking about pausing my schooling for a bit."

"How come?"

"I've gotten involved in an entrepreneurial endeavor with a few friends and it's going pretty well. It's demanding more and more of my time. So school might have to give way."

"What kind of *endeavor?*" Cassandra asked, turning her

body to face him more directly.

"Well, among other things, it's a Bitcoin mining company."

"Oh, Bitcoin! I don't know a ton about it, but I'm very interested. How did you get started in that?"

"Well, my best friend got his undergrad in economics, then rejected most of what they taught him and instead began studying something called Austrian Economics. That led him down a rabbit hole of learning, which brought him to Bitcoin, and he needed help from the technical side putting it together, so he recruited me and several others to help. It's worked fairly well so far and it's taking more and more of our time. But we absolutely love it and it doesn't feel like work at all."

Cassandra nodded, serious now, a tiny vertical line showing in her forehead. "I need to learn about Bitcoin. I've heard so much but know so little."

"The curiosity of the inner geek?"

"Precisely!" she answered, her accent again catching Marcus's notice.

Hours passed imperceptibly on that bench as they talked about their backgrounds, their family, their faith, and their friends. They shared stories and laughs until most of the crowd had dispersed and the sun was low in the sky.

Marcus eventually noticed the time and said, "Are you hungry? The Original Hot Dog Shop is calling my name."

"The 'O'?" Cassandra answered. "I love that place. I'm in. Should we walk?"

"We can, but I've got an electric bike we can ride. It's kind of a hybrid between a mountain bike and a motorcycle."

"Of course you do. That fits you perfectly. But can it fit two?"

"Er, I've never tried, actually."

"No time like the present," she said, already on her feet.

2

That autumn season saw Marcus and Cassandra growing closer. Their relationship flourished and they increasingly enjoyed each other's company. Pittsburgh was the ideal setting for their budding romance. They loved walking downtown, spending Saturday afternoons on the rolling lawns of Schenley Park, and visiting Phipps Conservatory and Botanical Gardens. For all of it they had the ever-present backdrop of the Pittsburgh city skyline; the buildings like tall soldiers standing at attention and casting mute approval. Marcus tried to teach Cassandra how to properly spiral an American football, while she countered with attempts at getting Marcus to juggle a soccer ball, which she called the *real* football, or *calcio* in Italian. They laughed and experienced many of those wonderful firsts that young love brings, and enjoyed discovering each other's peculiarities, foibles, and quirks. Cassandra, for instance, didn't like doughnuts.

"Who doesn't like doughnuts?" Marcus asked when she first mentioned it.

"*Moi,*" she replied with a shrug, demonstrating, like a true European, her flair with yet a third language. "But let's be honest, that's not as crazy as not liking dogs!"

"Hardly! But remember, it's not that I don't like dogs. It's that I don't want to own one. I don't get pets, in general, but particularly dogs. I mean, people treat them like members of the family, spend tons of money on them, let them sleep in their bed with them, lick them in the face, almost like making them surrogate children!"

"Listen, I know I'm not from around here, but I don't think most American children lick their parents in the face."

"You know what I mean!" Marcus laughed. "And when you go to visit someone with a dog, or worse, multiple dogs, they jump up on you, cram their noses in your crotch—"

"Wait, dog owners do this?" Cassandra interrupted.

"Ha! Very funny. No, the *dogs* do! And they, the dogs, just so we're clear, practically molest you while the clueless owner stands there and says something totally irrelevant like, 'Don't worry, he won't bite.' It's not being bitten that is usually the biggest worry at such a moment. It's that Fido there thinks I'm his new love interest!"

Cassandra laughed, knowing Marcus was mostly being extreme for entertainment's sake. And that was one of the things she liked about him best: his ability to keep her laughing and amused. Marcus, for his part, enjoyed her intelligence, curiosity, musical ability, and of course, her overall appearance, which had caught his eye initially.

"So what happens when you see a woman you find more attractive than me?" She had once asked coyly. "I mean, you say you saw me and 'just knew,' but that's pretty shallow, don't you think? Choosing someone based on her looks from sixty feet away? Don't get me wrong, I appreciate that you acknowledge my 'goddessness.'"

"You know that's not how it was!" he answered. "It wasn't about looks, although, well, OK, it was, uh, that's where it started, but it was more like something deep down inside me found a puzzle piece I had always been unconsciously seeking, and bam! There it was. Fully formed. The perfect fit!"

"Fully formed?" she smiled.

"Again, you know what I mean!"

"And I'm a puzzle piece, hand-crafted to fit into your life picture?"

"OK, when you put it like that it sounds self-centered and even chauvinistic. But you know that's not my heart. Whatever it was, as soon as I saw you, I had the deepest feeling that my life was lining up with something enormous, something destined, something infinitely right."

"I had some pretty strong feelings that first day, too. But the big question now, mister, is how you're going to fare without me for a whole month?"

"Do you *have* to go back to Italy for Christmas?"

"If you knew my family, you would never even ask a question like that. Papa is probably already at the airport waiting for me, two weeks early!"

"You could come to Michigan and spend the holidays with my family."

"I love your family, but I've already spent some weekends with them. Think about this: I haven't seen my family in person since before I met you! Doesn't that seem like ages ago?"

"Yes, actually, it does, in some ways. And for all the right reasons."

"Agreed," Cassandra said. "But I am very close to my family, as you know, and I miss them terribly. I can't wait to be back with them for the holidays. What we should be talking about is figuring out how you can go with me!"

"I know, I know. But there's just too much going on with the company right now. The guys need me, and there's no way I can take off that amount of time. Bitcoin never sleeps."

"I get it. But let's figure out how you can plan far enough ahead to come back to Italy with me next summer when school is out. Do you think Bitcoin would understand if you gave it that much advance notice?"

"Yes, my dear, it'll have to!" Marcus said in mock formality.

***

The holidays came and went, winter slipped into spring, and summer came quickly, with Marcus and Cassandra's relationship only deepening throughout. They had grown close, spending nearly all their free time together riding bikes, playing tennis, taking walks, watching soccer on an iPad (Roma was Cassandra's team), or even doing very little at all. It didn't seem to matter what they did as long as they were together. They were one of those low-drama couples that just seems to click. Marcus loved to listen as Cassandra worked through a song she was writing or as she learned a new piece on an instrument. She played her portable electric keyboard beautifully and wasn't too bad on the acoustic guitar. Marcus would sit on her couch with his laptop open, working on some challenge at his company, while in the background she would play the same portion of a song over and over again until she got it right. For Marcus it was like the soundtrack to their relationship.

Soon they began planning many firsts for Marcus: his first trip to Italy—his first trip to Europe, for that matter—and of course, his first chance to meet her parents. Cassandra was completing her junior year and was on track to graduate in one more. Marcus and his friends' Bitcoin company had grown. In roughly the same time frame that Marcus had fallen in love and gotten to know Cassandra, his business had consumed the rest of his time, and his studies were a thing of the past. But busy as he was, there was nothing that would keep him from this trip to Italy. For unbeknownst to anyone but himself, not even his parents or best friends, Marcus had bought an engagement ring. Someone who didn't know them might think it was too soon. After all, they'd been together less than a year. *But when you're sure, you're sure*, thought Marcus. Cassandra was simply the woman he'd dreamed of his whole life. He knew they were meant to be together, and he was certain Cassandra felt the same way.

His plan was to first make a good impression on Cassandra's parents, then officially ask her father's blessing to marry his daughter, and finally pop the question a few days before his trip back to the States. Marcus even envisioned that Cassandra's senior year could be utilized to plan a wedding for the following summer once she'd graduated. And his company should really be on solid footing by then, able to support them in whatever direction they chose to pursue life together. But all those details would fall into place after the big surprise of his proposal. One thing he had come to know about Cassandra; she loved surprises. He would spring the biggest one of her life in just the perfect setting right there in her homeland.

What could go wrong?

3

Cassandra had flown to Italy ten days ahead of Marcus and waited for him now at Fiumicino Airport just outside Rome. Marcus brushed his teeth with his finger in the tiny airplane bathroom and ran a flimsy comb through his hair in an effort to at least look presentable. He was jet-lagged and stiff from attempting to sleep while flying through the night, sitting up in a tiny airplane seat. Back in that seat, he glanced around at the other passengers and thought they all shared the same haggard appearance. Hair stood up awkwardly, clothing was rumpled, and items were strewn about. The flight had lasted just over eight hours and was the longest he'd ever taken. He eagerly peered out the window at the farming landscapes below as the airplane banked and lined up for final approach. The rising sun reflected off brown stone houses with tile roofs and lit up large, ancient looking parasol pines in rolling farms. Italy already looked very different from the American Midwest in which he'd grown up. Marcus was full of wonder about the coming weeks and could hardly contain his excitement. Mostly, though, he couldn't wait to see Cassandra.

She rushed forward from a disorganized mob outside the gates of customs, threw her arms around Marcus, and gave him a passionate kiss. She was wearing the same blue dress from the day they'd met.

"I can't believe you're really here!" she exclaimed, eyes twinkling. "My family is so excited about meeting you!"

"It's funny. This is the most important first impression I'll ever have to make, and I haven't slept, I'm jet-lagged, and I'm sure I look like a mess, while you look absolutely gorgeous!"

"Thank you, and you look fine. They're going to love you! Come on, let's go. I'm illegally parked." And with that, she grabbed his hand and pulled him out into the bright morning sunshine and the chaos of a busy international airport.

Cassandra talked nonstop in the car during the half-hour drive.

"My hometown, as I've told you, is Grottaferrata. It's part of the Castelli Romani, the 'castles of Rome.' They're the hills situated southeast of Rome in the Alban Hills. There's a crater from an ancient volcano up there, and today it's two lakes, Nemi and Albano. There are old Roman temple ruins all throughout the area, and even the Pope's summer residence, still in use."

The highway took a turn and climbed a long, gradual hill. Cassandra pointed and said, "Look, you can see it all directly ahead in the distance. See those tall hills with the buildings lit up by the sun? Those are Castelli Romani."

"Beautiful," Marcus answered, and leaned across and kissed her on the cheek. "I want to see it all! Don't let me miss anything!"

They drove higher through winding hills, narrowing streets, and traffic circles into a residential area. Tall umbrella pines cast blankets of shade against the warming sun. Stone walls surrounded and obscured many residences, and often a view of the expansive city of Rome was visible between buildings as they passed. Marcus thought it looked serious and important—somehow even wise—sprawled across its wide valley. But then, he was in a poetic mood. Everything was so old, solid, and permanent looking he could practically feel the history.

"How old are these buildings, roughly?" he asked as they passed an ornate church.

"Depends. Some are over five-hundred years old. Most are at least a few hundred. There is an old monastery right in my town, we're almost there, it's called Santa Maria in Grottaferratta or the Greek Abbey of Saint Nilus. It was founded by monks out of Calabria around the year 1000!"

"Amazing. Such history. What culture down through so many years and epochs. And you grew up in the midst of it all. Right here. Roots going deep."

"I think you're starting to get it," Cassandra smiled while turning the wheel sharply onto a side street.

They were perched up in the hills now, winding through skinny streets in what appeared to be a subdivision. Apartment buildings gave way to individual houses with tiny yards, each surrounded by brick and stone walls. They pulled in through a narrow opening in a rock partition into a short driveway of gravel fronting a two-story brick and stone house bordered by tall cypress trees. It had forest green shutters and an orange tile roof. An iron-rail balcony crossed the full front of the narrow house on its second floor. Dark wood-framed double glass doors with sheer drapes rustling gently in the breeze stood open onto a concrete stoop in the center of the ground floor. The house was just the sort of place that Marcus would imagine a loving Italian family would inhabit, and, as if to prove the fact, two figures emerged from the open doors.

"That would be my parents!" Cassandra said, grinning at Marcus as she yanked the emergency brake up into position.

Marcus was barely out of the car when a boyish man in his fifties with wavy dark hair gave him an enormous bear hug that almost lifted him from his feet, followed by an air kiss on one cheek and then the other. The scent of musky cologne wafted in the air.

"Marcus! My boy! Welcome to our home! *Come stai?* How are you? How was your flight? I'm Giulio and this is Cassandra's mamma, Stefania. Welcome, welcome. Come in, come in!"

Stefania, bearing amazing resemblance to her daughter, or actually vice versa, made her way to Marcus and gave him a gentle hug. "We're so glad you could come visit us!" she said. "Cassandra hasn't been able to stop talking about you. We feel as if we already know you! How was your flight?"

They made their way inside and Marcus was offered a glass of juice and some sparkling water, then given a plate of cheeses and olives. The questions and the chatter were constant, everyone talking at once and all seeking to make him comfortable and welcome. Then Giulio left the room for a moment and returned, leading a small black and white Havanese by the leash.

"We heard you don't like dogs, so we'd better get this over with sooner than later. This here is Crescendo. Nobody can resist her, right baby?" Giulio said, bending down to give the dog a loving rub on the head as he disconnected the leash.

Crescendo raced over to Marcus and stood up against his leg, wagging her tail and licking his outstretched hand.

"Uh, no, no problem," said Marcus, "It's not that I don't like dogs. I'm just not an enthusiast, that's all. And Cassandra has told me all about little Crescendo here. How ya doing, girl?" Marcus awkwardly made the obligatory overtures to the pesky little creature. Without invitation, Crescendo jumped up in his lap and curled into a snuggly ball.

"See. She likes you already! That's a good sign, eh?" said Giulio.

For the next hour Marcus was bathed in conversation and attention from Cassandra's parents. Crescendo wouldn't leave his lap, as if she alone had been elected by the dog world to win over this last remaining human to the general cause of dogs everywhere. Meanwhile, Cassandra's parents asked about Marcus's family, his faith life, his background, and all about how he had met their daughter. Marcus was very thankful they spoke English so well, and he inquired about how that came to be.

"Well, I went to university in the United States," explained Giulio.

"Really? I'm not sure I knew that. What's the story there?" asked Marcus.

"I had a soccer scholarship in South Carolina, but I also had a benefactor."

"A benefactor?" asked Marcus.

"Or a patron, yes, it was a tremendous blessing. Do you know the name Anthony Talamo Rossi, by chance?"

"Um, no, I don't think I do."

"He's the founder of Tropicana, you know, the orange juice company?"

"Oh! Yes, OK."

"After Rossi came to know the Lord, he would organize a crusade in the town of his birth every summer, using his fortune to spread the gospel. Well, that's my hometown, too. I got saved at one of those events, and shortly after that I got the call to preach. Rossi and I got to know each other, and he helped me with my education into the ministry. Again, using his fortune for the Lord."

"Wow!"

"Yes. So after university in the States, I returned to Italy and began my ministry. Stefania here learned English in school, and when we married, we decided that if God should grant us children, we'd raise them to speak excellent English by using it often in the home. That's what we did. That's why our Cassandra can almost sound like an American. Do you speak any Italian?"

Marcus flushed a little and said, "Not really, only a few words Cassandra has been teaching me. But I definitely want to learn it. You've heard the joke? What do you call someone who speaks multiple languages?"

Giulio and Stefania returned blank stares.

"Multilingual, or a polyglot," Marcus answered. "What do you call someone who speaks two languages?"

"Bilingual?" Stefania answered, catching on.

"Correct," answered Marcus. "And what do you call someone who speaks one language?"

Silence.

"An American!" Marcus blurted. "That's me, I guess. At least for now."

"Ah, that's good, good. Well, Italian is a beautiful language. You should really do it. You would enjoy it, too, I think."

Cassandra leaned forward and put her hand on Marcus's knee. "How are you feeling, are you tired from the jet lag?"

"A little foggy, I suppose. But I'm doing fine. Just glad to be here."

"Well, there are two approaches to adjusting to jet lag. One is to try and stay up until our normal bedtime here, or make it to at least nine o'clock or so. The other is to take a nap now, but not too long, and then get up and have dinner and again, retire at a normal time. Which would you like to do?"

"Oh, I think I'm good to try and stay up," Marcus answered, but he should have known better. Within a half hour he felt his eyes closing and knew he was losing the fight. Soon he was asleep on the couch, Crescendo curled up on the floor near him.

Cassandra and her parents slipped away to the kitchen.

"So what do you guys think?" she asked.

Giulio winked. "Yes, dear, he's a special boy. You did good. Good."

"We see how happy he makes you. That's what's important to us, honey," added Stefania.

"But what did you say about his business? He dropped out of school to do a business?" asked Giulio.

"You can't really say he dropped out, Papa. He is only a few credits short of getting his master's degree, after all. But he and some friends started a Bitcoin business. It takes up the time he would have used to continue his studies, so …"

"Bitcoin. I keep hearing about this Bitcoin, but I don't understand it."

"Maybe I'll let you ask Marcus about it, Papa. He's the best one to try and explain it."

"OK, sweetie," he said, planting a kiss on the top of her head. "I'm so happy for you and this young American Bitcoiner."

4

Marcus awoke with a start. He hadn't intended to sleep away the afternoon, but now it was dark outside, and he had no idea what time it was. He was still very tired and felt as if he could sleep for days. The house was mostly dark, too, so he listened for signs of life. He fumbled for his phone, but it had apparently been removed from the room with his bags. At that moment Crescendo ran in and leaped onto the couch, aggressively licking his hand.

"She sure likes you!" Cassandra said, flicking on a light as she entered. "How do you feel?"

"A little wonky, but not bad. What time is it?"

"Approaching eight. Are you hungry?"

"Starving."

"Great. If you're good with it, I think we're going to go out to dinner tonight. My parents want to take you to one of their favorite places."

"Of course I'm good with it."

"Ok, sweet, then let me show you to your room. Mamma has it all made up for you, and you can shower if you'd like. We won't leave for an hour or so."

"Dinner at nine?"

"It's Italy!" Cassandra answered. "And if it were Spain, we'd have to wait another hour still!"

Marcus emerged from his guest room feeling much fresher. He still sensed the drag of jet lag deep down, but on the surface he was bright and awake. The shower had helped. The smell of the delicious breads and sauces coming out of the restaurant kitchen a few feet away didn't hurt, either. But mostly, it was Cassandra and her doting parents that accounted for his excellent mood. Nothing could be more perfect, he thought.

Each course was ordered for him and explained in detail by an enthusiastic Giulio. There was pasta, salad, bruschetta, cheeses, chicken, eggplant, potatoes, and white beans. The owners of the restaurant and its staff were obviously friends with Cassandra's family, because upon entering there had been a full ten minutes of greetings and hugs and kisses for everyone all around, including those stirring pots over stoves in the back. And with each new plate that arrived there was banter and laughter before whomever had served it disappeared into the kitchen and brought back something more. Marcus wished desperately that he could understand Italian. Everyone seemed to know the Federicis and there was lots of enthusiasm for meeting Marco.

"So tell me more about your ministry," Marco finally got the chance to ask Giulio once the second plates had been cleared away and the food lectures had tapered off.

"It's best described as an itinerant ministry, I think. Though we're involved in a lot of things. Have you ever read the book *Rascal*?"

"Uh, no, never heard of it."

"You should. It's all about people who go against the grain, carve out their own path, march to the beat of a different drummer, that sort of thing. I only bring that up to try and make it clear for you, that I am kind of a rascal pastor. I mean, I am an evangelical Christian in a land of Catholics and atheists. I teach Jesus, but do it through the various outreaches of my ministry and many partnerships with other organizations throughout Italy. It's kind of hard to explain it all, but God has blessed it. I hope it redounds to His glory! And, this year marks our thirty-fifth. So God has been so good."

"That's great," answered Marcus.

"I can hardly believe it, really. Man. The time flies. Yes. That's one thing you will learn as you get older; the value of time."

"So you preach all over, in different places?"

"Well, a lot of time preaching, yes, and also some fundraising. The arrangement that we just kind of developed over the years is that I speak to churches and organizations throughout the United States, and they support the ministry. Then, when I'm in Italy, I direct the activities of the ministry and preach and teach at some events. But there are many aspects to what our ministry does. We form strategic partnerships with other organizations throughout Italy, and we distribute booklets to school children, get involved in response needs for national disasters, hold leadership development conferences, and try to serve local Italian communities in meaningful ways. We are a little bit unconventional, like I say, rascals, but we get a lot accomplished."

"Interesting. Would there be any ministry events I could get involved in while I'm here?" asked Marco.

"Yes, of course. Lemme see. In a few days I go down to

Napoli to check on the Christian House. It too is involved in many things, also, but right now is doing all it can for the refugees coming in from Africa. We're going to have an open-air evangelism in the public square. There are some local musical bands who will play, and a couple of the pizzerias are pitching in to feed everybody."

"I think I heard something about the African refugees coming into Italy."

"It's a big deal here, man. Really big. These poor people arrive here in the Bay of Naples with nothing. We are trying to feed them, give them some shelter, some resources, and of course, tell them about Jesus. They are so lonely and so distraught. It's a tragedy. Most of them have lost everything. There is a huge need."

Marcus nodded, realizing that his life was in sharp contrast to these unfortunate ones Giulio was talking about. He had a bright future, a comfortable home, a beautiful girlfriend he hoped would become his wife, and, and . . . his list of blessings tapered off as he lost his train of thought. He was incredibly tired and was vaguely aware of the fact that he should have answered Cassandra's father with something more than a nod. To his right, Stefania gently grabbed Cassandra's arm as a kind of signal, shifting her eyes toward Marcus at the same time.

"Ok, Papa, I think it's time we let Marcus get to bed. We can talk more tomorrow."

"I think I'm fine, really," said Marcus, playing it tough, while secretly wishing for nothing more than a bed.

"Maybe so, but it'll be better tomorrow if you get some good sleep tonight. Trust us, Papa has gone back and forth to the U.S. so many times he's got it down to a science."

"Yes," Giulio answered, "some sleep now would be good. But tomorrow, you must tell me about Bitcoin."

5

There was no time to discuss Bitcoin the next day or the day after that. Each morning Cassandra drove to the train station in Frascati and from there took Marcus into Rome.

"It's actually much faster to take the train into the city center than to drive," she explained.

They toured the ruins of Ancient Rome: the Forum, the Colosseum, Palatine Hill, the Mamertine Prison, and the Circus Maximus the first day. On the second they went through the Vatican Museums and St. Peter's Basilica. Marcus was mentally numbed by so many layers of history in one fabled city. Beautiful architecture, ancient culture, Renaissance art, and more were a lot to absorb in just two days' time.

"This place is overwhelming—like drinking Champagne from a firehose. It's magnificent," Marcus said. "And to think, you grew up around all of it. Does it ever get old to you? Do you ever find yourself taking it for granted?"

"I don't think so," said Cassandra, "I have always loved everything about it. But I think it's even more enjoyable having someone I care about to share it with. Especially when you appreciate it so much."

"That I do," he answered as they boarded the train heading

out of Rome.

They were both tired after walking all day and it felt good to sit down. Marcus set his bag of souvenirs on the floor between his feet and put his arm around Cassandra.

"So tomorrow we go to Naples to the Christian House?" he asked.

"I think I'm going to let you go alone with Papa. It will be a long day and I've got some stuff to do with Mamma that I promised her. Are you all right with that?"

"Of course. Though I'll miss you. But if I am imagining this correctly, your dad will be keeping me plenty busy anyway." Marcus was secretly pleased. His real reason was that a day alone with Giulio would give him the chance to ask for Cassandra's hand in marriage. He smiled inwardly at the thought. For Giulio had certainly been welcoming and nice to him, and he was confident the request would be a mere formality. Even so, Marcus was still nervous.

***

Giulio and Marcus left in the family's black Volvo station wagon early the next morning before the sun was up. Crescendo watched longingly from the front door window. Giulio noticed and said, nodding, "She likes you."

"Ha! Yes. Guess I have a way with dogs."

"But yet you don't like them?"

"Well, it's just not a love. But Crescendo is a really nice dog," Marcus said, knowing he was reaching.

After a moment, Giulio said, "My daughter is very happy because of you."

"Thank you sir. She makes me very happy too." *Now*, Marcus thought, *do it now*.

They drove on in silence for a moment, Marcus mustering his courage.

"Actually, sir, I wanted to have a little conversation with you."

Giulio looked sideways at Marcus in the passenger seat as they rounded the traffic circle and merged onto the A1 headed south.

Marcus decided to just blurt it out. "I am in love with your daughter. With your permission, I'd like to ask her to marry me."

Giulio was quiet and looked straight ahead at the road as they got up to speed. Marcus watched him, holding his breath. Giulio continued to accelerate until Marcus felt an anxiety growing inside. He noticed his palms sweating, and the speedometer rising through 160 kilometers per hour. Pavement raced under the car. Giulio swerved in and out of slower vehicles and still said nothing to Marcus. After an agonizingly long silence, Giulio slowly turned to look at Marcus, who worried that Giulio should be paying more attention to the road, especially at this speed. Marcus now felt layers upon layers of anxiety, his thoughts scattering like spilled marbles. Giulio's expression was stern and his voice a tone Marcus had not yet heard.

"I can't say this comes as a total surprise. But this is still a very big deal. You haven't even known each other a year."

"I know sir, but I—"

Giulio interrupted and nearly shouted, "I'm not finished," then drove on in silence long enough that Marcus could feel the discomfort like stifling humidity on a hot workday. Finally,

Giulio broke the tension and said, "I like you. Stefania likes you too. And it's plain to see that you make my daughter very happy. But she is our only child, my only daughter. She's very special, one of a kind. My little girl. We have raised her so carefully, with so much love. I have told her all her life that who she chooses to marry is the most important decision she will ever make outside of accepting Jesus. And here it is, right in front of her. Also, she is still very young. In Italy, we are not accustomed to giving up our daughters so early." He paused for a moment and focused on his driving, looking at the speedometer and deciding to speed up. "Let me ask you: Does she know you are doing this?" Giulio said, looking inquiringly at Marcus.

"No, sir. I didn't want to do anything without your blessing first," Marcus said, suddenly extremely glad he had decided to completely surprise Cassandra with this proposal. He couldn't imagine Giulio's wrath if the two of them had already made assumptions without his approval.

Giulio nodded to himself, looking back at the road. More silence. Then he said, "And you plan to live your life in America?"

Marcus paused, unconsciously wiping his hands on his pants. "I hadn't thought about that sir, but, well, that's not true, exactly. If I thought about it at all, I was assuming that, to be honest, yes, we'd live in the United States."

"You are asking to take my daughter away from me?"

"No. Sir. Not at all. I don't want to do anything to harm any part of Cassandra's family life. It's her close ties to you and Stefania that make her who she is, that makes her the woman I love. But yes. Geography is going to be a part of this."

"Ya think?" Giulio quipped, speeding up even more, and

making some kind of hand gestures to an Audi that wouldn't get out of the left lane fast enough for his liking. He mumbled *"Mamma mia,"* under his breath, and Marcus was amused that Italians actually said that. But his moment of levity quickly passed as Giulio continued.

"I can't give my blessing yet. Not at this time. No. It's too quick. Too sudden. This is too big of a deal. And I hardly know you. I don't understand what you do for a living, and this will mean my daughter most likely goes to live in the United States away from her mamma and me."

After this outburst, said quickly and without looking at Marcus, Giulio finally slowed down a trifle. But they were still the fastest car on the road.

Marcus felt his stomach tighten, and sweat beaded up on his forehead. He tasted rust in his mouth, and his vision grew dim as he squinted against the rising morning sun coming up over the mountains to the left of the highway. His nose was acutely aware of Giulio's cologne, and the scent of the upholstery in the car. And his mind reeled. This was entirely unexpected. After meeting Giulio and Stefania, he had really liked them. He felt they had liked him, too. If they were an American family, he thought, asking the father for permission to wed the daughter was just a nice formality. Marcus had to confess that he had assumed that to be the case with Cassandra's father, and had perhaps taken it too lightly. But yet, he had taken the correct steps. He had behaved honorably. His motives were pure. And he loved Cassandra and wanted to spend the rest of his life with her. Frustration welled up inside him, and then actual fear. What if he couldn't get Giulio's approval? What then? What would Cassandra say? Would he or should he even tell her? What should he say next, in these next moments, in this suddenly awkward and silent car ride?

Giulio seemed to be gathering himself, too. He adjusted how he was sitting in the seat and cracked the driver's window for some fresh air. At that speed, it whistled in violently. He turned on talk radio and Marcus, of course, understood none of it. Neither spoke for quite some time.

Marcus knew he had to do something. He struggled with what to say, like a man at his own trial. Finally, he managed to come out with, "Sir, I respect your position. I understand. And I just want to let you know that I will do anything you say to earn your trust, and ultimately your permission, to marry Cassandra. You say you don't know me? That's true. But I'm convinced that if you did, or, when you do, you will approve. I am convinced Cassandra and I were made for each other, and I'll do whatever I can to make you and Stefania comfortable with this. I am entirely at your mercy and will do whatever you say."

More silence followed, thicker than ever, and Marcus wiped his hands again. He replayed everything he'd just blurted out, trying to assure himself that it had sounded OK. But he was running on adrenaline now, dealing straight from the heart. He was playing no games and taking no chances. Or, maybe, he was taking the biggest chance of his life.

6

The rest of the drive was as silent as a snowfall on a Jerusalem Sabbath. Marcus had spoken straight from the heart, but Giulio had made no reply and stared fixedly at the road ahead.

Traffic increased tremendously as they neared Naples, and Giulio began talking again, as if their tense conversation had never occurred. He explained the history of the city, talked about its proud heritage in the Italian culture, and touched on topics ranging from poverty and population density to the Mafia who had for centuries been based in Naples and Sicily. Giulio himself was originally from Sicily, he explained proudly. Then he recounted the background of the Christian House and the fine young men who were his protégés who ran the place and had a real heart for people. And finally, way down in the lower part of the inner city, where they had pulled into a cavernous parking garage that was carved into the *tufo*, the soft volcanic rock, beneath the buildings above, Giulio shut off the car and turned to squarely face Marcus.

"Today is an important one. These people need our help, and we have to be at full attention to meeting their needs. As soon as we step out of this car, it is not about us. We must put our stress behind us and focus on them. Can you do this?"

"Uh, of course," answered Marcus.

"We will talk more on the way home about Cassandra. There. We go," he said, opening the door and climbing out.

For the next hour or so, Marcus struggled to do what Giulio had asked. His mind continued replaying the morning's conversation. Like a computer subroutine running in the background, much of Marcus's mental capacity was being used to churn the same issue over and over in his mind. But slowly, gradually, the interactions with the people and especially the refugees eased him out of it. The extreme helplessness of these people affected him deeply, and the love being shown by the group of young men running the Christian House was amazing.

There were introductions, hugs, air kisses, handshakes, and lots of conversation in the local Napoli dialect. It all sounded like Italian to Marcus, but someone mentioned that it was different, and that almost everyone around him was speaking it. A few of the people helping out at the Christian House spoke some English, but nobody spoke it anywhere near as well as Giulio and Stefania, and it was at first difficult for Marcus to communicate.

Some of the people being served by the Christian House, however, spoke fairly understandable English. At one point during the day, as Marcus assisted with the setup of a portable pavilion that would function as the bandstand for the musical groups that would later perform, Marcus struck up a conversation with the person helping him.

"Xavier," said the man, with a scrawny hand outstretched for a handshake. "I here two months. House helped me. You? American?"

"Yes, I'm Marcus. I come from America. A place called

Michigan."

"Mee-shee-gun," Xavier repeated, trying to pronounce it. He then nodded, and grinned.

"Yes. Have you heard of it before?" Marcus asked, speaking slowly and enunciating the best he could.

"Yes. No. I think so." Xavier smiled. His breath was bad. His clothes were worn. But his smile was wide and infectious.

The afternoon went quickly with Marcus and Xavier and many of the other volunteers and refugees all working constantly to set up everything in the sizeable piazza for that evening's festivities. Through broken English Marcus and Xavier chatted throughout the day. In some unofficial and unspoken way, the two sidled up as partners as they took on various projects and tasks assigned by the organizers of the event. Giulio checked up on Marcus periodically and introduced him to people throughout the day.

Later in the afternoon it rained, and people scurried for tarps to cover speakers, soundboards, and equipment. The rain intensified to the point that many were driven through the one door entry into the narrow and winding space that was the Christian House.

The place felt subterranean to Marcus, a boy from the suburbs of America, here in the deepest part of the inner city of ancient Naples. The Christian House—with an entrance one foot from the passing traffic on a narrow, one-lane street—was part of the ground floor of a tall building that seemed connected to buildings in every direction, each reaching high enough to block out the sun. Windows above it all had small metal balconies with clotheslines and women rushing to bring in garments before they got wet from the rain. To Marcus, it looked as if it

must be a city-wide laundry day. Small cars and scooters and
mopeds buzzed by closely and constantly in both directions,
and Marcus was quite sure he had never been anywhere so cha-
otic in his life.

As they took shelter inside the Christian House, crouching
against a damp wall on the concrete floor of the main hallway,
Xavier and Marcus made use of the time to talk. Xavier introduced Marcus to many of his acquaintances. Each explained,
through Xavier's translation or through elementary English of
their own, which country they were from, what they had done
as a profession in their homelands, and what had transpired
to drive them to Italy. Marcus was drawn into their plight and
amazed at their warmth and eagerness to connect. As the day
wore on he could feel their pain deeply within himself more
than he ever had for anyone or any cause. It was as if something
inside had burst, like the blue bag in an emergency cold pack,
changing his temperature toward tragedy in a way that could
never be reversed. But instead of cold, it was warm, even hot.

Eventually the weather cleared, tarps came off, and the piazza filled with people. Pizzas flowed from the portable ovens
as the bands played loudly, and the atmosphere grew festive despite the heavy humidity that hung in the air and pressed down
like a physical force. People hugged, laughed, and talked inces-
santly in multiple languages. There were old women perched
on stools and folding chairs and children running and darting
among the adults. Men gathered in clusters and smoked and
talked and slapped each other on the back, laughing and gestic-
ulating with more hand motions than Marcus had ever seen. As
it grew dark the music stopped and someone at a microphone
introduced Giulio. He ascended the small platform under the

awning Xavier and Marcus had earlier erected and began to preach. The noise from the group abated a little, but the chaos was so strong nothing could have quelled it. Giulio was unrelenting, though, and wouldn't be distracted. He spoke on through it all with evident passion and tenderness, his words projecting from the speakers and echoing off the aged buildings encompassing the square. It was obvious to Marcus that Giulio knew his territory and his craft, although Marcus could barely understand a word. People were noticeably touched by what Giulio said. Marcus observed tears, nods, and murmurs of approval. After he was done, Giulio led a group prayer, then left the platform as the music cranked up again.

Z

The return trip to Grottaferratta didn't begin until well after dark. Marcus was drained both physically and mentally by all he had experienced. His legs ached and his joints were stiff, and he nursed a cut on his left hand he had received from one of the brackets on the gazebo they'd assembled. But the much older Giulio appeared as spry as ever, taking the wheel and navigating the crazy Naples traffic with the same aggression he had shown on the A1 highway heading down that morning. Eventually, as the traffic thinned and they once again entered the highway, Giulio turned to look at Marcus.

"What do you think of today?" he asked.

Marcus hunted for words. His emotions were many, and he searched for the right response, taking his time. "I am overwhelmed. I'm feeling much pain, on behalf of those people. I am even feeling anger."

"Anger?" Giulio asked, eyebrows raised.

"Yes. Anger. Do you know Xavier, the tall, forty-ish man whom I was with for much of the day?"

"Yes, I believe I know the one you mean."

"Well, he spoke fairly good English, at least better than most of the others, so we were able to communicate quite well eventually. At any rate, his story really touched me. Did you know that he was a tenured college professor back in his country?"

"It doesn't surprise me—" answered Giulio.

"And he introduced me to people who had been dentists, doctors, professionals, engineers, you name it, all having their lives destroyed by forces beyond their control. And here they are barely hanging on, hurting, most of them having lost their families. What's more, they have been stripped of their identities and any professional credentials. They have no way to prove who they were or what they are able to do. And this is all besides the lost money and property. I guess it's hard to take. It makes me feel soft, wimpy, spoiled . . . I don't know. I just don't have the words, I guess, Giulio. But let me say this." Marcus swallowed hard and considered his next words carefully, not wanting to flatter, but feeling his heart full. "I am very, very impressed by you and your young men back there, the Christian House guys. You are all doing a very important, and good, work. Thank you for letting me be a part of it today. Honestly. Truly. I don't think I will ever be the same."

"I am glad you came along. Know this, Marcus: our privileges are not for our pleasure, but for our purpose. The world has it backwards. But as believers, this is how we are to act." Giulio was then quiet for a moment, once again, and driving just as fast as he had on the way down that morning. Somehow, this time, Marcus barely noticed. Then Giulio said, "Tell me more about this anger."

"Oh! Man! I'm not sure I want to talk about it. It will just make me madder yet."

"I want to hear."

"Well, do you know what happened in Xavier's country? Do you know what started the collapse of his society and the total destruction of that man's life!? It was the government mismanaging the country's currency, as Xavier explained it, which led to hyperinflation. This led to financial ruin for many, including Xavier, as the government changed hands in one military coup after another, each regime bloodier than the previous one. The breakdown in their money ruined their economy, which caused a total collapse of law and order, as well as of all the other structures of a civil society. Xavier is an educated man. He knew what was going on. And there was nothing he could do to stop it. And here he is now, alone, his family killed in a needless bloody war, and him washed up on a foreign shore and hanging on by his fingertips. Thank God for people like you and the Christian House. Without you I don't know what he and the others would do!" Marcus actually had tears in his eyes.

Giulio nodded, and a look that Marcus could only read as approval came across his face. But interestingly, Marcus wasn't all that interested in Giulio's approval anymore. He was interested in justice, in helping, in making a difference and doing something meaningful in the face of so much suffering. The last person he was thinking of at the moment was himself.

Marcus continued. "You said you didn't understand Bitcoin. Well, I can tell you, Bitcoin was created to fly in the face of just that kind of injustice. It was meant to sever a relationship that should never have been allowed: specifically, government being in the money business. Lord Acton once said, 'Power corrupts—'"

"And absolute power corrupts absolutely," Giulio interrupted and finished for him.

"Exactly. Putting the unlimited power of money creation and supply in the hands of self-serving governments is a recipe for—and I mean this now more than I ever have meant it before—disaster! Governments over the years have been diabolic enough to move money away from anything sound, anything that will hold its value. They moved it away from silver and gold and cleverly, in complicated ways, moved it into something called fiat money, where a government's currency is only money because they say so. They demand that you pay your taxes in it, and force you to accept it as legal tender. As a result, people work their entire lives for it, expending the best, most precious, healthy, and energetic days of their lives in exchange for it. It's a con in which people swap the most precious and finite thing they have—their time—for worthless paper which is abundant and can be increased indefinitely at the stroke of a computer key. Because just like that," he snapped his fingers, "the government can create more, instantly. Because what happens, what *always* happens, is they can't keep their hands off the so-called printing press, and they make more and more of it, to their benefit, and at the expense of the people in what is essentially an invisible and regressive tax. When people work, they are exchanging their limited and precious time for money whose quantity increases all the time. They are trading infinite value for counterfeit value, which itself gets devalued. It's infuriating."

Giulio nodded. He was listening intently and driving even faster.

Marcus continued, "When governments expand their money supply—and this always happens with fiat money because there are no limits to how much they can put in circulation—it debases the value of the currency already out there in circulation. This means that if anyone has the audacity to actually save some money, to set aside some of the fruits of their hard-earned labor, it actually decreases in value. It goes down in value over time, because of what the government is doing by their self-serving tampering with the supply of money. And even more so by what banks are doing by getting everyone addicted to the global drug of debt, which expands the money supply also. And, get this, through controlling the educational systems, people are taught only one type of economics, the type that blesses everything governments and banks do in their monopolistic money practices and debt money binges, and this effectively blinds people to what is really going on. People even get to the point where they think that prices increasing over time is a natural, normal thing!"

Giulio nodded once more and looked at Marcus, saying nothing but studying him intently. Marcus could swear Giulio hadn't looked at the road in over a mile, and in some kind of mental game of chicken, Marcus concluded it was important to maintain eye contact and not ruin the moment. So despite the feeling of impending highway doom, and the unrelenting need to look forward and make sure they weren't about to hit something, he stayed still and glared right back into Giulio's eyes.

It must have been the right move, because suddenly Giulio turned back to the road, looked at his speedometer, and slowed down awkwardly as if even he himself were startled at their speed. Then once again he turned to Marcus. "OK, Marcus. OK. I propose we make an accord. And by an accord, I mean an arrangement that is even stronger than what you Americans might call a deal."

Marcus waited silently, his heart beating with pronounced power, his breathing slow, eyes firmly on Giulio. He had no words, and was unsure of what was coming, but again, he told himself to remain silent and just let Giulio talk. Giulio reached over and turned off the distracting talk radio that had been blaring throughout their exchange so far. The new silence added to the drama Marcus felt.

"I propose . . . I propose . . . that . . . well, first of all, I want to inform you that Stefania and I have always told Cassandra three things about the man she would marry someday. Number one," he said, raising a finger defiantly, "he must love the Lord Jesus with all his heart and above everything else. Number two," he continued, raising a finger to join the first one, "he must love my daughter completely and unreservedly. And number three," he said, again raising another, "he must love his own family. Cassandra has, of course, told me all about you. And further, I've observed you and listened to you these four days, but especially today, and particularly in your words just now. And I do believe you satisfy all three, or I wouldn't be about to say what I'm about to say." Then he stopped talking and looked back at the road, his forehead creased and his body leaning forward. Marcus sat silently, afraid to move or breathe, anticipating what would come next.

Giulio finally continued, "OK . . . here it is . . . the accord . . . I propose, that, OK, I will give you my blessing to marry Cassandra, *if*, and I mean only *if*, in the remaining two weeks you are here, you convince me, and explain Bitcoin and how it works and that it is a good idea. If you can do this—if you can convince me, teach me, and explain it to me in such a way as I can understand it completely and have as much passion for it as you do—then, and only then, and only *if* you do this, no wiggle room, you understand? *If* and *when*, then, well, then, you can propose to my Cassandra."

8

Marcus felt tears in his eyes once again, but now they were tears of happiness instead of indignation. He looked at Giulio but couldn't speak. Giulio nearly smiled, but the hardness of his face quickly returned. Marcus noticed a service station, one with the odd-looking logo on the sign featuring a wolf with seven or eight legs.

"Um, can we pull in there please? I need a pit stop."

Giulio shrugged and put on his blinker.

Inside the restroom Marcus splashed water on his face and tried to get control. The day had been beyond emotional, and now this. He needed a clear head. He needed to proceed carefully. And he needed help.

Reaching into his pocket, Marcus removed his cell phone and dialed an international number. It rang several times as he quickly calculated the time back in Pittsburgh. Sometime after lunch, he concluded, just as a voice answered.

"Hello? Marcus. What's up, man?" said the voice.

"Ari, hello, boy, am I glad to hear your voice. I've got a crisis."

"What is it? Are you OK?"

"Yeah, yeah, sorry, it's not an actual emergency. I'm going

to ask Cassandra to marry me."

"Hey, congratulations! That's great, man! Really! You two are a model couple. Everyone says so! But how is that a crisis?"

"Well," Marcus replied, "it's kind of complicated. You see, it's her old man."

"Uh oh."

"No, no, no, he's actually really great. But he's plenty old school, if you know what I mean. And get this—long story—but he won't give me permission to ask Cassandra to marry me unless I convince him about Bitcoin!"

"What?"

"Yeah, seriously, I've got to convince him about it."

"Convince him of what?" Ari answered.

"I mean, explain it to him. Teach him about it, in such a way that he really gets it. That he not only understands it but becomes like us—totally sold."

"Ah, OK, that's a little weird."

"You don't know the half of it! But please, I'm serious. This guy doesn't mess around. He's the real deal, which isn't surprising, really, considering the daughter he and Stefania raised."

"Is Stefania her mom?"

"Yeah."

"She a babe like her daughter?"

"Ari! This is serious! I'm calling secretly from a bathroom in Italy, for crying out loud!"

"OK, OK, sorry dude. But is she?"

"Ari!"

"OK, sorry. What do you need me to do?"

"How would you suggest I go about it? I mean, we have to explain to people what we do all the time, but never in this kind of a circumstance, never with this much on the line. I just don't want to blow it and I thought of you, right away. You're always so good at teaching people about it."

"OK, dude, relax. You've got this. You can do it. I'll tell you this much right now, you have to begin with the reasons why. People get all confused and distracted by the computer science and the cryptography. Or they get sidetracked by the price action and the lure of something for nothing. But none of that will make any sense, or have any meaning whatsoever, until someone truly understands the *why* part of it. Only once you explain the *why*, should you dive into the *what* and the *how*."

"So begin with economics," Marcus said, not really asking.

"Yes. Money. You've got to start with money, what it is and what it's not. How it's broken. This is the practical way to explain Bitcoin. You have to help people understand the problem that it was created to fix."

"Yeah, yeah, got it."

"And listen, Marcus, I'm going to text you a bunch of links to stuff that might be helpful memory joggers and good summaries of things. You can either use them to review yourself or just give them right to, er, what's his name?"

"Who?"

"Cassandra's dad. Man, you really are in a panic."

"Giulio. His name's Giulio."

"OK, Giulio. You can give plenty of references and articles to Giulio if it helps. But just start with first things first. See how that goes, then call me."

"OK, this is good for me to hear. I mean, there's just so much that we know, we've got the curse of knowledge, I'm not sure how to sift out what's important from what's not important. I don't know how to take someone from zero all the way up to a clear understanding. I mean, if you think about it, money and computers are two areas that most people don't understand much about at all, even when they think they do. And Bitcoin is a mash of both!"

"I know, dude, I know. That's always the challenge."

"*And* I'm under a time pressure. *And* there is a lot at stake!"

"I get it, Marcus, but you'll be fine. I gotchoo. And Cassandra can help you, she's a very smart cookie."

"No, actually, she can't! She doesn't know anything about this. I've got it all set up to be a big huge surprise. She loves surprises and I don't think she sees this coming. Well, yes, she does, eventually for us, I mean, but I don't think she would ever suspect it on this trip, this soon, the first time I am meeting her parents."

"Oh man, that's a wrinkle. So she can't know at all about what you're trying to accomplish with her dad?"

"Nope, not for the way I want this to go down and to preserve the surprise."

"Alright. Hmmm. Then you really are on your own over there. But don't stress, you can ring me any time. I'll make myself extra available and I'll do my best to pick up if I see you calling in."

"You're the best, Ari. Thanks. And I'd better get going. I've been in here a long time."

"See ya, buddy. Good luck."

"Thanks. Ciao!"

Ari hung up the phone and thought, *Ciao?*

Marcus re-entered the car and Giulio looked at him with a raised eyebrow. "So," he asked Marcus, "are you ready to explain Bitcoin to me now?"

"Like my wife depended on it!" Marcus quipped, to which Giulio actually smiled.

2

OK, here goes," Marcus said as they merged back onto the highway. "Bitcoin is a fascinating invention, a transformational technology, a super-cool computer science experiment, and a whole host of other things, but we wouldn't be talking about it right now if it hadn't come along as a proposed solution to a significant problem, or problems."

"You said government money," Giulio said, and Marcus knew he was listening and tracking.

"Yes. At the highest level, the problem is that people don't even know there is a problem. What I mean is that things have been arranged in such a way, and have been that way for a long enough time, that people just accept it. But the status quo is unjust, is a silent scam, and is doing real, actual harm to people. Money is broken. Witness Xavier and his country's collapse. That's an extreme example, but fiat money tends to run to extremes."

"Fiat money being the dollar and the Euro and the like," added Giulio.

"Yes. Fiat money is based on the Latin term *fiat*—"

"Which means 'let it be done'" interrupted Giulio. "Italian is based on Latin."

"Yep. It is money that is simply money because a government declares or decrees that it is and forces us to use it as such. It is backed by nothing except the might of the government decreeing it. And fiat systems are subject to tampering. In fact, there has never been a fiat money that didn't get debased."

"You may not realize what I know about this part," said Giulio. "I lived through the transition from the Italian lira to the euro. Brussels really raked us Italians through the coals, man. They declared what the value of the lira would be in exchange for their new money, and that was it. Take it or leave it. Actually, we had no choice but to take it. And if you measure our purchasing power against the dollar, before and after, we lost a huge amount. It was very, very hard on our ministry."

"Yes!" said Marcus. "That's the thing with fiat money. Governments, through their central banks, can just haul off and do that kind of arbitrary stuff and people pay the price."

"Experiencing it first-hand teaches you that lesson," said Giulio. "And let me tell ya, you never forget it. A Sicilian never forgets, man! It's power; that's how it works. It always centralizes. How could they put us in that vice and squeeze us like that into the euro in such a bad deal? Centralization. A big, centralized power amassed against us as individuals. It's always the same principle being violated."

Marcus continued, "Yes, precisely! I called my friend Ari, who is an economist, he is one of the ones I'm in business with, and he is sending me some material I can give you. Right here on my phone he just texted me this list of just some of the extreme train wrecks of fiat currencies, which I totally agree with you, are only possible through centralized control: the Papiermark in the 1920s in Germany, the Argentinian Peso in the

1980s, the Peruvian Sole in the nineties, the Zimbabwe Dollar in the 2000s, the Venezuelan Bolivar in the 2010s, I think you get the idea. All of these currencies got expanded more and more by their governments until they experienced hyperinflation and they became worthless. This is what happens with fiat currencies."

"All of us Europeans know about what happened to Germany between World War I and World War II," Giulio said. "Their hyperinflation caused so much damage to the people. It brought down their society, really, and is what allowed someone like Hitler to rise to power."

"Exactly! That's the kind of stuff that happens with fiat money," Marcus chimed in. "And this is going on today. The supply of US dollars expanded 26 percent in the year 2020 alone. 26 percent! And people don't realize that there's a problem, which means they are easy victims of a system designed to serve itself at their expense. And here is the way that works: central banks regulate the money supply, and they do so through a mechanism that creates debt. No new debt, no new money."

"Debt."

"Yes, debt. Let's take the US government, for example, because I'm the most familiar with it. But it relates almost directly to the behavior of the European Central Bank as well, which you live under. The US government famously spends way more than it takes in in tax revenue, so it has to borrow to make up the difference. It does this by issuing what are essentially IOUs to the Federal Reserve, or Fed for short, which in everything except name is the central bank of the United States. It gives these IOUs, called government bonds, to the Fed, which 'buys' them with money made out of thin air that gets deposited in the

Treasury for the government's immediate use. This is all digital, so it is as easy as creating digits in a computer. When people say 'printing money,' yes, there are some literal printing presses making actual paper money, but not much. These days most of our money is digital. 'Printing money' is shortcut terminology for creating new money out of thin air by this process of bonds issued by the US and sold to the Federal Reserve. It's just digits put into a computer. I'll probably use it throughout the rest of our conversation on Bitcoin. The main thing is this: we have government able to create unlimited amounts of new money out of nothing in order to meet its hungry spending habits."

"Doesn't sound like a good idea," Giulio said. "That's an unlimited power, no?"

"Exactly. The so-called 'regulation' of this money supply is done behind closed doors by appointed elites and then reported to the press in veiled and complicated terms and presented as though it's normal and just. The effect of this ability of the world's governments to create digital money out of nothing is that all of their currencies grow in circulation—meaning as they create more and more dollars (in the case of the US), there are more and more dollars out there in circulation, and that lowers the value of the dollars that are already out there, making them less valuable for buying something. All the dollars are fighting for the same products, and the more dollars there are, the higher the prices for those products go. And as you know, this is called price inflation."

"Yes," said Giulio, "and when it gets really out of control, that is hyperinflation, as in the case of Germany I just mentioned. The best way I ever heard it explained, young Marcus, was this way. Picture this: You and I go to a collectors' car auction, and there are a lot of other people there who all want to buy this one particular car, say a Lamborghini Countach. Suddenly, someone comes in the room and silently slips each of us would-be purchasers an extra 1000 euro. Now, everyone in the room has an additional 1000 euro than they had before. As a result of this, what do you think will happen to the bids we give for that Lambo?"

"They will go up," answered Marcus, nodding.

"Correct. And likely they will go up by as much as 1000 euro or more each, so correspondingly, the price of the car will go up. More money chasing the same quantity of goods equals higher prices. If that's the case, then what happened to the spending power of the euro we already had with us? It went down. They were *devalued* by the influx of new money into the situation."

"Yep, exactly right," said Marcus. "That's a fantastic explanation, Giulio, I'm going to use that. Now, imagine this. Take the illustration one step further. Picture that just moments before we are ready to begin the bidding, someone invites in another couple hundred people into the process, except these new people are not given the extra 1000 euro that we received. What happens to their likelihood of being able to win the Countach at auction?"

"It goes way down."

"They got scammed by the fact that some of us were first in line for the new money. Well, this is what happens when a government creates more money for itself out of thin air, *it gets to use the money first.* Prices haven't moved yet because there haven't been any of the new inflationary dollars in circulation yet, and the closest people or entities to the new money creation stand to gain the most benefit from it. There is a term economists use for this—the Cantillon Effect. The government and the people closest to government spending gain the most value from the money created. So number one, this unlimited printing of new money is unfair to anyone who has accumulated some savings of that money which is now losing its value, as your Lamborghini auction illustration showed, but then number two, there is an incentive for people to get near the game and snuggle up to those who run the printing press, so to speak, which is unfair to all the people who are not privileged to do so."

"Wow," Giulio said, holding the vowel and displaying his Italian accent.

"Governments publicly act concerned about the growing gap between the rich and the poor, but right there at the heart of their money-printing scheme is a regressive situation, meaning it favors the rich and disfavors the poor. This is because the first ones to get the benefit of the new money are rich financial institutions and government contractors and the like—all run and controlled by big money interests.

"But hold the phone, because as bad as all that is, governments aren't even the biggest creators of new money, regular banks actually are."

"They are?" asked Giulio.

"Yes. Oh, and one of the books my friend Ari just texted me to remember is called *Exposed: The Financial Matrix* by Orrin Woodward. That book explains all of this better than anything we have ever come across, especially this part. Banks, when they loan money to people for houses and cars and student loans, are expanding the money supply too, and actually to an even larger extent than the central banks of governments do! The process is called *fractional reserve banking*. Banks take deposits from people and then loan out nearly the full amount of these deposits to other people, who then deposit some of that money which mostly gets loaned out too, until the growing spiral of debt through this repeated lending is many times greater than the original deposit that started it all. Again, it's just digits in a computer, and they are allowed to do this when the government grants them a banking license. A banking license essentially says, 'You are granted the power to loan people money that doesn't exist and then charge them interest on it.' This expands the money supply like crazy, which devalues the money people already have. Just as in the car auction, this makes prices go up. The *Exposed* book has charts and graphs and tons of amazing smoking guns in it that will show you just how big the con has gotten. Debt is like a drug, and banks have gotten rich by getting people hooked on it."

"I'll get that book," answered Giulio. "The author's name is Owen Woodward?"

"Orrin. O-R-R-I-N," answered Marcus. "But I'll get it for you; don't worry about it. I can't recommend it enough as the best definition of the problem that Bitcoin came to solve."

"Thank you. I'll definitely read what this Owen guy has to say."

"The bottom line is that the world's centralized financial system, built on debt issued from both central banks and regular banks, in the form of fiat money, with no limits or checks on the amount of its creation, invisibly robs people of the hard-earned fruits of their labor. It serves governments and those with close ties to governments at the expense of the people and encourages recklessness in government behavior and spending, which leads to funding all sorts of things the people would never vote for, like endless wars and enormous self-serving bureaucracies, and is a tool of control. Governments and the banking system are joined at the hip in a coordinated game of exploitation that is mostly invisible to the honest person working hard each day to make a living—not to mention the surveillance , lack of privacy, discrimination in lending, risk of confiscation of funds, bailouts and bail-ins, the redistribution of wealth, and all the other injustices and encroachments on freedom that are also built into this system of centralized government money."

"That's a mouthful. But I am already convinced of all of this, Marcus. Remember, I'm a Rascal. I understand and cherish freedom and am wary of ever trusting the state to have its hands on the till."

"Then you are a Bitcoiner already, we just haven't finished the initiation process."

"We'll see about that," answered Giulio, his eyes focused hard on the road ahead.

10

"OK, I won't get ahead of myself," Marcus continued as they drove along. "The first step in all of this is to realize that money is broken. It is centralized in the hands of governments and banks who serve themselves at the expense of the people. What makes all this possible is the fact that fiat money is disconnected from anything of value, and its supply is strictly under the control of governments who want and need to spend it, and banks who want and need to lend it."

"Whoa, I've never heard it said that way," said Giulio.

"Things weren't always this way. There is a money that emerged during the human experience that wasn't fiat, that wasn't made by any government and couldn't just be printed in larger and larger quantities or loaned out in an endless mathematical expansion."

"You're talking about gold, of course," answered Giulio.

"Exactly. You see, people have been living under a fiat system so long they are now practically unable to see or conceive of anything but a fiat world. They've been gaslighted into thinking all of this is normal, healthy, and correct. But money isn't something that just belongs by default or by right to the government. In an uninhibited theatre of human action, or free market, money emerges on its own. The decentralized mass of individuals making their own decisions are capable of selecting a tool to use to serve as their money. They don't require a government to dictate to them what it should be. And over the centuries, they selected gold."

Giulio nodded. "Because of its scarcity."

"You got it. It emerged as a natural money in the free market of human interaction largely because of its scarcity. And even more important than gold's scarcity is its scarcity *over time*, meaning the supply of it doesn't change much from year to year. It is very hard to mine more of it, it's very expensive to do so, and the supply of new gold has a hard time reacting to an increase in demand for it. This property is known in economics as inelasticity. The more disconnected supply is from demand, the more inelastic something is. It is explained by something called the 'stock-to-flow ratio.' How big is the stock of something compared to how much new of that same something can be found, mined, whatever. Follow?"

"You bet," said Giulio.

"A low stock-to-flow ratio means that a lot of that item is readily produced compared to what's available already. A high stock-to-flow means very little new supply is produced compared to what's already available. Still with me?"

"Sure."

"So it's this high stock-to-flow that ultimately is what made gold such a good choice to be used by people down through the centuries as money. Its value was very stable, what economists call 'sound,' or 'hard,' because its supply was extremely limited and therefore the above-ground stock was pretty constant over time. When you work hard and want to store the value of some of the fruit of your labor, and save it over time, in essence, to pass it forward through time to your future self for later use, then you want something that holds its value."

"Incidentally," chimed Giulio, "governments did find ways to cheat with gold, even as far back as the Roman Empire. They would melt pure gold and mix in cheap alloys that couldn't be detected, or plate worthless metals with gold on the outside, or clip little shavings off the edges of coins, that sort of thing. In this way they could pass off a certain amount of gold as if it were more than it actually was."

"Exactly!" said Marcus. "Effectively they were devaluing the money just like fiat central banks do today. As a matter of fact, those who advocate for a return to a gold standard miss this. A gold standard ultimately never worked for long because humans always debased it. It had to be centralized, which led to manipulation. But in terms of gold itself, it is pretty hard to tamper with. It's not subject to the whims of central bankers, and it's apolitical. Gold is gold. And that made for good money. At least, until Bitcoin, the best money man had yet found."

"I've always wondered what happened from then, when the world used gold, to today, when the world is all on fiat money?" asked Giulio.

"Way back, gold was very valuable, of course. The goldsmiths who worked with gold on a regular basis were accustomed to having some on hand and having to store it securely. They soon began storing it on behalf of other people. They issued receipts for the gold on deposit, and eventually people began trading the receipts. Instead of going to get the gold in order to spend it, people simply began spending the receipts themselves. These, of course, could be used to redeem the gold from the goldsmith at any time, but were much more convenient and transportable than gold. It didn't take long for goldsmiths to realize they could get away with giving out more receipts than gold they actually had on hand, since it was very unlikely all of the people would come and ask to redeem their receipts all at once. This was the beginning of fractional reserve banking we talked about a few kilometers back."

"Yep."

"Then, as governments gave themselves the sole right to mint and coin money within their realm, making it illegal for private banks and individuals to do so, they at first used gold to back their paper currency. This backing gave it a reference value. Citizens could redeem these paper 'demand notes' for the equivalent amount of gold. In the United States, the government decided to abruptly stop this practice, and even passed a law to make the holding of gold by individuals illegal! They actually confiscated the people's gold. Therefore, at that point, the US was almost on a completely paper fiat money system, except they still allowed foreign nations to redeem *their* demand notes for gold. When nations began doing this in the late 1960s and early 1970s, the US didn't have enough gold on hand to redeem all the notes that were coming in, because they had already expanded their money supply way beyond what they held in gold reserves. Essentially, the US wanted to spend more money than it had to finance things like the Vietnam War and the Great Society welfare programs. So President Nixon closed the gold window, effectively telling the nations who wanted to redeem their dollars for gold to pound sand. After that, there was nothing to stop the money printer from going *brrr.*"

"So when these nations tried to redeem their dollars for gold, it was like all those people in the ancient villages with receipts all going to the goldsmiths at once demanding theirs," said Giulio.

"Exactly right. Nixon simply disallowed any further re-demptions, saying it was temporary. Of course, as Ronald Reagan once said, 'There is nothing so permanent as a temporary government program,' and in the case of this one, it was half a century ago and is still in effect. Basically Nixon said, 'Sorry folks, park's closed. The moose out front should have told ya!'" Marcus said in his best imitation of John Candy's famous line in the movie *National Lampoon's Family Vacation.*

At this, Giulio laughed out loud. "I love that movie!"

Marcus smiled, realizing for the first time he was actually enjoying the process of discussing this enormous subject with his potential future father-in-law. Giulio already appeared to have a very good understanding of money and the financial world, and that was making it easier, to be sure. But Marcus had begun to realize what a great bonding exercise this might turn out to be and was thankful for it.

"From then on," Marcus continued, "the US dollar was tied to nothing, backed by nothing. Today, the entire world follows that example and runs on fiat money."

"But we were talking about gold." Giulio leaned forward over his steering wheel. "Governments and central banks still hold gold. No matter how hard they try to make us believe their money is sound, their actions show the truth. As the old saying goes, 'What you do speaks so loudly what you say I cannot hear.'"

"Absolutely. Their vaults are full of the stuff," said Marcus, looking down in reaction to the buzzing of his pone. "My friend Ari just texted me this: 'The world's central banks bought more gold in 2018 than they have since 1967.'"

"Almost like they are preparing against the inevitable crash of paper money," nodded Giulio.

"We're left to conclude little else," said Marcus. "And for years, people have themselves been exchanging some of their paper currency for gold in order to try to save in a way that won't be devalued."

"Yes," nodded Giulio.

"But there are some challenges with gold. It is difficult to move around, especially in large quantities. When Germany decided to bring back $31 million worth of gold stored in the Federal Reserve in New York and in a vault in Paris, it took over four years and cost $9 million to do so. That's the problem on the big side.

"On the individual, emergency side it's not much better. Imagine if Xavier had somehow tried to escape his country with some gold. Somewhere along his dangerous journey to Italy, you know someone would have stolen it, or even killed him for it. By the way, not to jump too far ahead on you, but with Bitcoin, Xavier could have left the country with all of his wealth simply stored in his head. With Bitcoin, if you memorize a handful of what are called *seed words*, you can use them to access your Bitcoin anywhere in the world whenever you want. It will also be possible for someone's credentials to be securely stored on the Bitcoin blockchain, and therefore Xavier's identity, too, would have been preserved. Imagine the implications for that in the interest of human freedom! Imagine how different Xavier's life would be right now if he had direct access to his former money and credentials."

"That's truly amazing!" said Giulio, clearly considering the implications of such a possibility. "There has never been anything like that, ever."

"Correct. It's just one of the many huge things Bitcoin brings to the world."

"Incredible," Giulio repeated, shaking his head.

"But back to gold. Gold is difficult and even dangerous to move," Marcus continued. "It's also difficult to store safely. It can be confiscated by governments, as in the case with the US government in the 1930s, lost in theft, or in wars, and it can be costly to assay, meaning, to verify that it is truly gold. Also, it's difficult to divide it down into small denominations. To buy a cup of coffee, for instance, would require a little tiny shaving."

"Ok, what does gold have to do with Bitcoin?" asked Giulio.

"One of Bitcoin's most important and perhaps biggest uses is as a *store of value*. It's like a digital version of gold, but with some advantages over gold. Some people call it 'Gold 2.0,' meaning, an improved version of gold. Bitcoin was intentionally designed to be scarce and have a very limited stock-to-flow ratio—even more so than gold—especially over time. Its total supply is fixed. There will only ever be twenty-one million bitcoins, and almost 90 percent of those have already been issued. And some estimates say that as much as 20 percent of bitcoins have been lost! The issuance of new bitcoins will run out around the year 2140. Further, since it's digital and can be subdivided down into super tiny denominations, eight decimal points, to be precise, someone could buy or spend a one-one millionth of a bitcoin, which is pretty small!"

"What's that worth, for instance?" asked Giulio.

Marcus opened the calculator app on his phone and tapped away at the screen. "At today's market price for bitcoin, in dollars, it's roughly 5 percent of one US penny."

"A very tiny slice."

"That's the beauty of digital. But it's also easy to verify. It is easy to send anywhere in the world. It is easy to hide, as we said about someone such as Xavier memorizing a few simple words. It can't be confiscated. There is no need for a central trusted party like a bank or a government to be involved. It cannot be censored, meaning nobody can tell you that you can't use it or limit how much you can use. And also, it is easy to store. We'll get into how these things are done later, but for now, the big thing to comprehend is that Bitcoin embodies many of the store-of-value properties of gold but in a digital form. And importantly, it improves on gold in some critical ways."

"This is all interesting, but I have more questions than you've given me answers," said Giulio, turning off the highway. "Let's stop for a coffee. It's been a long day."

11

Marcus and Giulio returned to the car after a coffee break at another highway station featuring a wolf of many legs on its sign, and Marcus marveled at the way even such little things were foreign to him. There were so many pleasing differences in Italy, and he was enjoying them all. Back home in the States, a coffee break would likely have involved a couple of large foam cups and a return to the car to drink while driving. In Italy it meant standing at the coffee bar and gulping from tiny ceramic cups on saucers while they talked. The difference was slight, but part of the overall pleasing aspect of unfamiliarity that international travel opened to him.

Refreshed, they continued down the highway.

"So in summary, so far," Giulio began, "Bitcoin was invented to be an alternative to the central banking system that currently runs the money world, and a more valuable, more functional store of value than even gold. Am I tracking correctly?"

"Yes, sir. You've got it. Half the problem with understanding Bitcoin is realizing the problem it was designed to fix. I think it's no accident that it was released into the world in January of 2009, immediately after the Financial Crisis. In some of the original communications written by its creator, the bailing out of central banks was clearly given as a motivation for its launch."

"Who created it?"

"A pseudonymous person, or persons, we don't know, who used the name Satoshi Nakamoto. There has been rampant speculation as to whether this was a man, a woman, or a group of people. Nobody knows for sure. And then, after a couple years of working online and through emails with other developers to debug the early versions of the Bitcoin software, this Satoshi person disappeared."

"Really?"

"Yes. And this turns out to be very important."

"I can easily see why. If this is truly such a disruptive invention and is on offer to the world as an alternative to its corrupt fiat money system, then this Satoshi person would be in danger."

"Yes," answered Marcus, "quite possibly."

"He could awake with a bloody horse's head in his bed!" said Giulio.

"*The Godfather*," said Marcus.

"Yes! See, in Italy, we have three books on leadership; Godfather Part I, Godfather Part II, and Godfather Part III," Giulio said with a grin.

Marcus shook his head smiling.

"But go on," said Giulio.

"Well," said Marcus, "not only do we not want any bloody horse heads, but there's another benefit from Satoshi's disappearance. Bitcoin is decentralized, meaning there is no person or group controlling it, no company backing it, no organization responsible for it. It now exists totally autonomously, on its own."

"Ah," said Giulio. "So this Satoshi disappearing was a big part of accomplishing that."

"Correct. No founder. No single point of failure. No trusted central party. No center at all."

"Brilliant, I think," said Giulio.

"Me too."

"And he's never resurfaced?"

"Only once, it seems," answered Marcus. "The authorities in the Unites States found an elderly gentleman with a similar name and accused him of being the creator of Bitcoin. After massive disruption in this man's life and an investigation, it became quite clear that his name was an unhappy coincidence. And, at that time, the real Satoshi, we think, made one last communication assuring everyone that they had the wrong guy. Beyond that, nothing."

"Maybe he's dead," said Giulio.

"It's possible. You can't believe how much speculation there has been as to who this mysterious person or persons is or was. But as time goes on and his invention survives and even flourishes, surviving attack after attack and mystifying its critics, his identity becomes less and less important. The critical thing is that he disappeared and left us a truly decentralized system without any single point of failure. It's this property that gives Bitcoin much of its unique ability to be what it is."

"Wow. A mysterious founding, an anonymous genius, an unsolved disappearance. It sounds like Hollywood stuff!" said Giulio.

"Truth is stranger than fiction, as they say. And although

his disappearance has been mythologized, and even seen in retrospect as part of his genius and almost like a benevolent step necessary to Bitcoin's ultimate decentralized uniqueness, it may have been that it just simply outgrew him. Many of the Bitcoin forum communications from back then do not indicate that people at the time were idolizing him. Early on he was certainly shown some reverence, but many people on the forums and in that development community were also using pseudonyms, so he was just thought of as a normal guy. But as the project grew and thousands and thousands of people got involved, it was much like any open source development project, with argumentation and disagreements and people taking shots at him or questioning his authority, and identity. Most open source projects kind of proceed under the tumultuous leadership of a benevolent dictator. In this case, that's how Satoshi operated. He would make changes unilaterally sometimes and contradict himself at others. Then as the scene grew more contentious, he kind of patched things up as best as he could, found a successor to assume leadership of the growing Barbarian horde that were coming into the project, and suddenly just stopped communicating entirely."

"Fascinating."

"It is. And I think Bitcoin is actually a bit different today than Satoshi might have envisioned. Perhaps. His early writings and communications seem to indicate that he wanted Bitcoin to be an easily spendable transactional money, what's called 'peer to peer,' in addition to this whole store of value thing we've been discussing throughout this car ride. But it has evolved more and more to be Gold 2.0, as I said, which is a bit at the expense of its scalability as a transactional medium. And of course, there are lots of opinions all over the board around these issues. You can imagine how calamitous a leaderless, truly decentralized project like this can be."

"It's an incredible creation story, no? Even the fact that it took flight on its own even once its initial creator lost control of it or let it go or whatever."

"100 percent," answered Marcus.

"So I think I am clear on the problem Bitcoin was created to solve. And that origin story is super interesting. But I am not clear on *what it is.*"

"Ok, that's the perfect next question. The simplest answer is that *Bitcoin is the invention of decentralized money.* It does this as a software program that runs on a network of thousands of computers, and it relies on the precision of mathematics instead of the goodwill of centralized institutions."

"So it's software. There aren't actually any physical coins?"

"Correct. It's all digital."

"What are these photos I see online and on the finance TV channels of a shiny coin with a capital B turned sideways on it?"

"Those are just props people have made to symbolize the idea of Bitcoin. Actual Bitcoin is just software running on computers."

Both men were silent for a moment as Giulio navigated the roads that Marcus now recognized as being near the Federici home.

"The invention of decentralized money," Giulio muttered to himself, as if suddenly understanding the gravity of what that phrase implied. Marcus remained silent.

"So it's not the invention of digital money?" asked Giulio.

"No. Digital money already exists. It's what most of the money in the world already is. Digital money is today mostly just a computer form of the fiat currency in which the world is drowning. Bitcoin might be the world's first *entirely* digital money, but that's really beside the point."

"OK, this is our neighborhood," Giulio said turning sharply into a corner on a hillside. "We can pick this up tomorrow."

12

Cassandra was at the door as they entered the house and hugged her papa first, then Marcus. As Giulio headed upstairs, Marcus and Cassandra settled onto the first-floor couch. Behind them the wall was covered in framed and faded photographs of ancestors.

"I missed you," she said, pulling her legs underneath her and moving into his side. "How was the day with my dad?"

"You wouldn't believe me if I told you!" Marcus answered, his mind reeling.

"That bad?"

"No, not bad. It was astonishing, really. Entirely unpredictable from the beginning to the end." He smiled inwardly.

"But good?"

"Yes. And let me tell you, that Christian House project was awesome. Have you been down there? Have you seen what they are doing? Been to any of their events like what I went to today?"

"Yes to all. I love that place. And Papa is very involved mentoring the guys who run it. They all look up to him tremendously and follow his input very much."

"Well, they're doing some impressive things. And those

poor people. Some of them spoke decent English and I got to hear their stories. Heartbreaking."

"Yeah," Cassandra nodded. "I love your big heart," she said softly, drawing in closer for a kiss. "Tomorrow we have nothing planned, so feel free to sleep in. You've had a big day."

Exhausted from the day's exertions, and drained emotionally on many levels, Marcus readily agreed.

***

The next morning Marcus and Cassandra discussed the day ahead with her parents as they savored fresh coffee from the town center. Crescendo lay at Marcus's feet throughout the conversation and periodically raised up to lick his hand.

"If you kids would like," said Giulio setting his cup down, "we could drive down to Lake Albano today, have lunch at Victor's by the shore. You'd like it, Marcus, it's farm-fresh and made from animals and items grown right on the premises." Giulio kissed the gathered fingertips of his right hand in a dramatic gesture.

"And then maybe we could take him up to Rocca di Papa," said Stefania. She was looking sharp in a flowery summer dress and cosmetic jewelry. Marcus had the quick thought that he had yet to see her when she wasn't made up and looking ready to strut in front of cameras.

"That's the Pope's official Summer Residence," Cassandra explained. "Lots of old-world charm and history."

"It all sounds great to me," said Marcus.

They spent an hour touring the area by car, pointing out sights and attractions to Marcus with obvious pride. Rome was occasionally visible on the valley floor miles in the distance, glistening in the sun under remarkably clear blue skies. At other times they got glimpses of one of the two crater lakes, deep below the ridge lines along which they drove. The Federicis showed Marcus a towering umbrella pine five-hundred years old that had necessitated a pronounced bend in the road in order to leave it undisturbed. They drove him to a location on a roadway through the woods on which the car, placed in neutral, appeared to roll up the hill instead of down. Many explanations were given for this, none of which made sense to Marcus, so he made a mental note to search it later on the internet. Next they descended from the ridges around beautiful Lake Albano and pulled into a gravel driveway between a low-slung restaurant building and a large pavilioned seating area, both offering a commanding view of the lake. They parked on the grass near some olive trees in the rear amongst free-ranging chickens and tethered goats.

"You see, Marcus? Fresh! See those vegetable gardens over there?" Giulio motioned his arm toward the large rocky hillside that ran along behind the property. "It's what feeds the table here at Victor's."

They entered the restaurant through the kitchen at the back, hugging and kissing and chatting with everyone along the way. Marcus was introduced several times and did his best version of the double air kiss-hug combination. Eventually, they arrived at a table in the front corner window that was evidently their regular spot. Sunshine angled in through windows which were cracked-open at the bottom, allowing the inflow of a gentle breeze smelling of flowers.

"Ah, the good life, eh Marcus?" said Giulio as they settled

around a rectangular table covered in a red and white checked cloth upon which already sat a basket of bread sticks, which were more like cracker sticks.

"Everything is so nice here. What a place to grow up!" said Marcus, imagining Cassandra's childhood.

"You're going to love the food here," added Stefania, and she went on to describe some of the more noteworthy dishes.

Giulio gave some instructions to the waiter while Stefania inquired about Marcus's day in Naples. Marcus explained what he had seen and experienced and expressed admiration for the work of the Christian House and Giulio's involvement with it. Cassandra beamed. She looked so beautiful Marcus wished he could propose to her right then and there. She caught his look and blushed a little, but held his gaze, and he thought he could read 'I love you' in her eyes. Marcus felt more determined than ever to win over Giulio.

"Ah, here it is!" exclaimed Giulio with gusto as the *antipasti* arrived. There were several plates of potatoes with melted mozzarella and prosciutto. Next came mozzarella wrapped in bacon. This was followed by Giulio's favorite: frittata with arugula and a blend of cheeses. Each of these was shared family-style, with large portions doled out for Marcus. All throughout this onslaught of culinary delight came explanations from the three Federicis about what the food was and how it was made.

As pasta with mushrooms, bacon and grated Romano cheese arrived, Giulio suddenly said, "Marcus here has undertaken to explain to me Bitcoin."

Marcus was caught unprepared and froze. He scrutinized Giulio, waiting for what would come next. If the business of convincing him about Bitcoin wasn't to be a secret from Cassandra, then Marcus could perhaps enlist her help, without her knowing, of course, of the overall objective.

"Oh yeah?" said Cassandra. "That should be fun."

"So far so good," said Giulio. "But we've got a long way to go for this old brain. At this point, we've really only covered the economics and the reasons behind its creation. But I must admit, Marcus has my attention with it."

"It must be strange having a profession that is so challenging to explain," said Stefania, offering him some more frittata.

Marcus slid the steaming triangle of food from the offered plate onto his own and nodded. "But that's also part of the fun of it," he answered. "It wouldn't be a leading-edge disruption if it was already widely understood."

"Marcus and his friends have had a very good start to their company," added Cassandra. "I'm sure if anyone can help Papa understand it, it's him."

"Well, this afternoon, most of the places around here will shut down for siesta. I propose we head back to the house and fix up some nice refreshments, and Marcus can continue my lessons."

"I'm game," said Marcus, more motivated than ever to get this done and get that ring on Cassandra's finger.

"We have a hammock in the backyard out by the olive trees that is calling our names," Cassandra said in Marcus's direction. Then, turning to Giulio, she said, "When Marcus is done with you, Papa, I claim him next."

13

Comfortably situated in folding chairs on the small back patio, Marcus and Giulio sipped sparkling water and looked out across olive trees in the backyard, or garden as the Federicis called it. Birds chirped and flitted about among the trees. Marcus was certain he had never been more stuffed after a meal. The lunch at Victor's had been delicious, to be sure, but he'd also found it impossible to say no to the continuous portions of food pushed in his direction. He decided that if time allowed, he would start taking morning runs for the rest of his time in Italy. Having thus eased his guilty calorie-conscience, he turned to the issue at hand.

"So Bitcoin," he began.

"Yes," replied Giulio. "Please let's continue with the lessons, oh Master of the Coin."

"Ha! Tesla!" said Marcus.

"Yes! I may not know much about Bitcoin yet, but I did notice in the news and think it was peculiar when Tesla, a huge multinational corporation, bought a gob of Bitcoin and gave that funny title to one of its finance guys."

"That Tesla move was an interesting chapter in the history of the adoption of Bitcoin," said Marcus.

"I figured."

"Yes. Its acceptance has gone from being an obscure project in the hands of a few cypherpunks to billions of dollars of it being purchased for corporate treasuries. All this in just over a decade. Pretty incredible. So where did we leave off, in your mind?" asked Marcus.

"The invention of decentralized money," answered Giulio, and Marcus knew from this that Giulio was truly comprehending.

"Yes. Money for the people that runs on its own. *Freedom money*, to use a term lots of Bitcoiners use. To summarize, then: what the internet was to communications and commerce, many are coming to believe Bitcoin will be to money. It's the best money technology that has ever come along. Its decentralization is a critical feature, because it is not in the hands of any central power. Bitcoin belongs to the people, not to any authority. It's an alternative to central banks and their fiat money. It's like a giant decentralized bank in the cloud that's open to everyone but controlled by no one. And because of its scarcity, and the decreasing rate of new coins produced, which we'll discuss in more detail soon, it is the hardest and soundest money ever known to mankind. For this reason, it is a tremendous store of wealth."

"So how does it actually *work*?" asked Giulio.

"Yup, I suppose that's next. We started with the *why* of Bitcoin, then the *what*, and now it's time for the *how*."

"Finally."

"Ha, yes. Which to me as an engineer is the most interesting part. But it can also be the most obscure and hard to explain, so I'll do my best."

"You'll do fine. Remember the prize," Giulio said with a raised eyebrow.

Marcus took a deep breath and started in. "Before I dig into the how, let me just say that understanding at least a bit of the inner workings of Bitcoin is important because it will help clarify all the properties that Bitcoin has. You'll see why people believe in it so much, why it has worked so well, and why it has never been hacked. So if this gets a little technical, remember that it's worth it. OK?"

"I'm ready," said Giulio with a slight mock bow.

"The problem at the base of fiat currencies is all the trust that's required in order to make them work. Satoshi himself wrote that. You have to trust the banks, you have to trust the politicians and the government, you have to trust all the middlemen who have a part in the game. In contrast, Bitcoin is a 'trustless' system. Bitcoin relies on mathematical certainty instead of faith in institutions. One person can interact with someone else directly, without anybody in between them making it possible. And the software is open source, which means anyone can read the actual code, and make changes to it. Of course, for those changes to get implemented there has to be vast agreement across the whole network, but we'll talk about that later, too. For now, it's important to understand that everything is open for everyone to see, so there doesn't have to be any trust even in how Satoshi created it. You can see for yourself how it works, and verify that there are no time traps, back doors, or special deals."

"OK, I'm following."

"So the first challenge Bitcoin had to solve was the elimination of 'trusted' middlemen, and it did so by creating something called a *peer-to-peer network*. The way it works is that each computer that downloads and runs the free Bitcoin software program becomes a 'node' in the system. All the nodes talk to each other constantly, with no moderator in between. Bitcoin nodes communicate with one another in what is called a 'gossiping network,' meaning that there is no hierarchy among the nodes, so each operates equally. When a node learns about new transactions on the network, it gossips about it to its peers. As every node connects to multiple peers, this information will generally reach every node in the network eventually. Through a process we'll get to in a moment, one output of the Bitcoin program is a *ledger*, or a public recording of all the transactions that take place on the network of all of these nodes."

"OK, what do you mean by a transaction?" asked Giulio.

"Let's say you send me one bitcoin. That is an example of a transaction. Any time someone sends any amount of bitcoins or fraction of a bitcoin, that is what constitutes a transaction in the Bitcoin system."

"Got it."

"Is there a paper and pencil handy? For what we're diving into, it might be helpful for me to draw some things out."

"Yes," answered Giulio standing up and heading into the kitchen. He returned shortly with a lined yellow legal pad and a mechanical pencil and handed them to Marcus.

"So all the nodes keep an updated copy of this ledger, which contains all the records of the accepted transactions," Marcus said while he sketched.

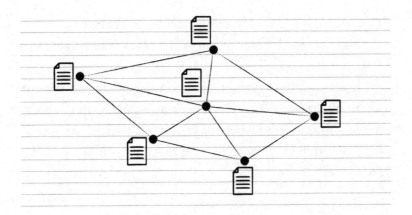

"Outside of Bitcoin, transaction ledgers are centralized, like in a bank or by a government, kept, maintained, and guarded by the bank or government's security protocols.

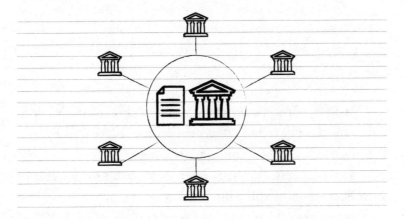

"But on the Bitcoin network, every node keeps its own copy. Because this ledger is spread all over the place instead of in one location, it's called *distributed*. And because no central party is in charge, as we've discussed a lot, it's called *decentralized*.

Those are slightly different terms, and both are important."

Giulio nodded, "This ledger is the blockchain, right? I've heard that term a lot."

"Exactly. The blockchain is appropriately named: it's just a chain of blocks of data, each block being made up of all the transactions that have happened all the way back to the launch of Bitcoin and its original starting block, which is called the *genesis block.*

Genesis Block   Next Block

"As new transactions take place, they get assembled into a new block of data and connected on the ledger to the block that went before it. A chain of blocks. See?"

"So far, I guess. But what is involved in these transactions, such as me sending you a bitcoin?"

"When you do so, there is some information that goes along with that action. There is the *amount* you are sending me; there is the *information* about you the sender and the info about me—the recipient; there is a *time stamp* of sorts; and a *fee* associated with this transaction. All of that makes up the data for this transaction between you and me. It's the data from transactions just like this one that gets gathered up, put into a block, and attached to the previous and most recent block in what becomes the official record of all the transactions on the blockchain."

"Who does all this gathering of transactions?"

"That is done by something called *miners*," said Marcus.

"Which is what your company does, right?"

"Yes, among other things. A miner is a particular type of node on the Bitcoin network, which means it's running a specific part of the Bitcoin program. What the miners do is scour the network for transactions. They automatically select a bunch of them and assemble them into a block of a certain size, which is called the block size limit. They are in a race with other miners who are doing the same thing. Whichever miner can 'win' this race earns the privilege of writing his proposed block as the next block in the chain. For doing this, they earn a *block reward* of several new bitcoins, newly minted by the Bitcoin program, from a part of the program called the coinbase."

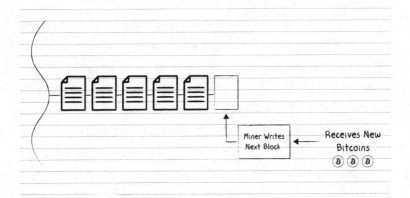

"So that is where new bitcoins come from?" asked Giulio.

"Yes. Brand new bitcoins that never existed before are given to miners every time they add a new block to the blockchain. And that transaction itself, the reward of those new bitcoins, is written as one of the transactions in that new block."

"So this is why you hear about miners using very specific types of computers and burning up a lot of electricity, because they are racing?"

"Correct. It's analogous to motorsports racing, I suppose, in which engineers and mechanics constantly seek ways to add horsepower to their motors in order to go faster and beat the competition. That's essentially what Bitcoin miners are doing," explained Marcus.

"I have heard it said that these miners are solving math problems or puzzles. What kind of puzzles?"

"Well, I don't know if puzzle is the right word. What the miners are actually doing is something more akin to rolling giant dice. Let me see if I can use an analogy for this that might help illustrate it.

"Envision a huge, enormous room with desks set up in rows and columns as far as the eye can see. At each desk sits one accountant with a pad of paper in front of him. Also on each desk is an enormous multi-sided die. These accountants are my analogy for miners. So picture this: All the accountants in that enormous room each hear about thousands of transactions taking place on the network. What follows are the steps they take in their race against each other: First, they select a transaction that happened out on the network, make sure it follows all of the Bitcoin program's rules—particularly that bitcoins aren't being spent that were already spent, that kind of thing—and for every transaction that follows the rules, they write it down on their ledger in front of them. Then they do this with another, as quickly as they can. And again and again. As soon as they can fill a page with these approved transactions, then they start rolling the huge die on their desk. On the wall of the gym there has been posted a giant tote board displaying a number. That number is called the *target number*, which is automatically generated by the Bitcoin software program each time this game is played. The first accountant who has filled a page with approved transactions and is then able to roll his die and get a number *below or equal to* the target number wins. As the winner, he gets to take his paper up to the wall and tack it to the next place in the chain of previous winners' papers. He gets to write the next block onto the chain. Does my silly analogy make any sense?"

"Yes, I think so."

"Good. Now picture that as each accountant wins a particular race and gets to tack his sheet of paper, or new block, onto the wall's long chain of previous blocks, then he is given some brand-new bitcoins from the Bitcoin program as a reward for winning that round. The blockchain grew in length by one block, and new bitcoins were issued automatically by the Bitcoin program as the prize. This awarding of new bitcoins for each new block written is the incentive for these accountants to play the game in the first place."

"OK."

"Next, picture a separate ginormous room filled with auditors sitting at each desk. As soon as a new paper or block is affixed to the chain of previous papers on the wall, meaning as soon as a new block is added to the blockchain, each of these auditors gets a copy of that latest block on his desk and begins checking it for errors. If it is error-free, then each auditor dutifully adds the new block to their own copy they are keeping of the blockchain on their desk. If the new block doesn't check out, they simply ignore it and don't write a new one onto their own ledger until one that is error-free shows up. With me still?"

"Yes, I think so. Who are these auditors?"

"They are what's called *full nodes*. This is just a certain part of the Bitcoin program that anybody can run on their computer. You can download the Bitcoin software onto your computer and run the full node program, and it will non-stop perform the job of an auditor like I've described. In this way every full node keeps its own copy of the growing blockchain."

"Is there a reward to them for doing this?"

"Well, there is no payment in bitcoins. Only the miners get bitcoins awarded for their work. But auditors, or full nodes, do this to not only support the Bitcoin network but also to have some benefits like having a wallet on the network in which they can keep their own bitcoin, that kind of thing."

"So who gets to be a miner, if that is where the new bitcoins are, doesn't everybody want to mine?"

"Great question. And yes, in the early days of the Bitcoin program, every computer running the Bitcoin software was a full node *and* a miner all in one. But over time these activities got specialized so everyone agreed to change the code and make them separate. Part of the reason for this is that mining became a more and more expensive race, demanding higher and higher powered computers just to compete, and it was useless to work one's regular computer that hard when it had no chance to win against the faster racers."

"So who can mine?"

"The short answer is that anybody can mine. All you have to do is choose to run a mining node in the Bitcoin software, but to do it profitably requires specialized computers, or connecting your computer to a bunch of other people's and pooling your resources. But we'll get into that later. So anybody can mine, but it's a specialty thing now for super high performance machines."

"Alright."

"Now, are you ready to dig down into the actual thing that's going on in this race between miners? I don't want to proceed unless you've got the idea in your head of my huge room filled with desks of accountants."

"Yes, I've got that cartoon fixed in my head."

"Ok, then let's unpack what they are actually doing."

"What who is actually doing?" asked Cassandra as she stepped out onto the patio.

"Young Marcus here is teaching me about Bitcoin mining," said Giulio.

"Well, I call a recess!" said Cassandra, taking Marcus's hand and guiding him to his feet. "That hammock beckons and Bitcoin can wait."

Marcus smiled at Giulio, shrugged, and followed Cassandra across the lawn.

"Thanks for rescuing me, honey. My brain was about to explode," Giulio called after them.

14

So you and Papa sure seem to be hitting it off! You looked like a regular couple of buds out there sipping your water and talking nonstop," said Cassandra in the hammock, one leg outstretched to touch the ground and gently swing.

"Ha, well, he wants to learn about Bitcoin."

"That's him showing an interest in you. He's good that way. He's always very focused on others. It's also a good sign, I think. It means he likes you," she smiled, poking him in the chest.

"I hope so."

"I'm so glad you were able to come visit and meet my family. I can tell they both like you. I don't know if I've ever been happier. I love you," she said, kissing him softly. They talked a while longer before settling into a comfortable nap, shielded from the afternoon sun by the dappled shade cast by the silvery leaves of the olive trees.

That evening the four of them were in the kitchen rolling out pasta, making sauce, and baking bread. Marcus had almost no cooking experience, so Stefania hung an apron on him and good-naturedly began bossing him around. In no time he was covered with flour and enjoying both the process and the banter. Giulio and Stefania told the story of how they met, teasing back and forth and interjecting with exaggerated kisses and terms of endearment. Marcus was struck by how affectionate they were and appreciated seeing a good marriage. They were also funny, in a boisterous way, and Marcus enjoyed that too. But most of his attention was on Cassandra. He loved seeing her in her home environment, in the warm embrace of her family. She was so beautiful and endearing to him that he couldn't wait to make her his wife. She smiled at him and flirted across the kitchen and he thought his heart would burst. *Nothing could ever be more right than this*, he thought.

The dinner conversation was a lively continuation from the preparation in the kitchen. The chatter never stopped, and neither did the food. It seemed that every meal was a contest to see who could get Marcus to eat the most. Once again, as the evening wore on, Marcus found himself stuffed to the point of discomfort.

As they finished cleaning up the mess together, Giulio said, "Cassandra, do you mind if I borrow young Marcus here and ask him some more questions about Bitcoin?"

"Sure Papa. I'm going to go up and do some reading. Marcus, let me know when you're done and I'll come back down," she said, giving each of them a kiss, Papa first. Marcus and Giulio settled into chairs at the kitchen table.

"I've got the picture of this enormous room with the accountants in it, representing Bitcoin miners," said Giulio.

"Good. Did that make sense?"

"Yes, I believe so. And then there's this other huge room with the auditors in it, representing the full nodes."

"Right."

"And those full nodes are just computers running the Bitcoin program, doing what they do automatically?"

"Exactly," answered Marcus.

"But what I am wondering is, what is this big die that the miners are rolling in order to play the game or win the race, or whatever, to be able to add the next block in the chain? What are they actually doing?" asked Giulio.

"So, I'm going to repeat myself a little bit here, but I think repetition will help. These accountants, which are my analogy for miners, remember, first gather up the transactions they hear about on the network, and then form them into a block. They do this until they reach the block size limit. Then the game they play isn't really throwing some giant die, in reality, it begins with them using something called a *hash function*."

"A hash function?"

"Yes. This is a pretty specific, sophisticated computer algorithm that takes data in one side and spits it out the other in a scrambled format. You could take something as small as one single alphanumeric character, or as large as the whole dictionary, either one, or anything in between, run it through a hash, and come out with a string of digits that—in the case of Bitcoin—is a predictable 256 bits in size every time, which are displayed as a sixty-four-character alphanumeric output. The particular hash function Bitcoin uses is called *sha256*, 'sha' standing for *secure hashing algorithm*, and the 256 representing the output size in bits. Still with me?"

"Yes."

"Do you know what bits are?" asked Marcus.

"Better tell me."

"OK, do we still have that paper and pencil?"

"Yes," said Giulio, reaching behind him.

Marcus spread the paper out before him. "Computers, at their deepest level, deal in ones and zeros, which actually represents a switch being either closed or open. Just two positions are possible, and just a one or a zero represents those positions. Transistors, which are at the very deepest heart of a computer, are just collections of billions of switches. So the number system with just ones or zeros is called binary numbers; because there are only two of them, one and zero. Binary. So for any bit in a computer, it's value can be either a one or a zero.

"The math for it looks like this: two possible outcomes per bit, to the power of one, because in this first example we are only looking at one single bit. So the total number of possible outcomes is two.

$$2^1 = 2 \text{ Possible Outcomes}$$
(either a "1" or a "0")

"It would work similarly if we had two bits instead of just one. There are still only two possible outcomes per bit, but now to the power of two, because now we are considering a two-bit result, so the total number of possible outcomes is four.

$$2^2 = 2 \times 2 = 4 \text{ Possible Outcomes}$$

1 or 0	1 or 0		1	0
			0	1
			1	1
			0	0

"Continuing, if we had three bits. Still two possible outcomes per bit, to the power of three, because now we are considering a three-bit result, so the total number of possible outcomes is eight.

$$2^3 = 2 \times 2 \times 2 = 8 \text{ Possible Outcomes}$$

1 or 0	1 or 0	1 or 0		0	0	0
				0	0	1
				0	1	1
				1	1	1
				0	1	0
				1	0	0
				1	1	0
				1	0	1

"So if we had the same two possible outcomes per bit but we're considering a 256-bit result, we would have a huge number of possible outcomes."

Marcus opened an app on his phone and looked something up.

"I'm actually going to write out the exact number so you'll see it. That crazy looking huge number represents all the possible different outcomes.

$$2^{256} = \text{115,792,089,237,316,195,423,570,985,008,687, 907, 853,269,984,665,640,564,039,457,584,007,913,129, 639,936 Possible Outcomes}$$

"So that's the first thing to know about the hash function that the Bitcoin core program runs: it generates an absolutely gigantic number of possible different outcomes. This is the mammoth multi-sided die that I used as an analogy," said Marcus.

"Wow. So when you said a big die with many sides, you meant that impossibly large number of sides?" asked Giulio.

"Ha, yes," answered Marcus. "Now, there are other features about hash functions that are important to what's going on here, as well.

"First of all, the output is *deterministic*, meaning you always get the same output for the same input. So if you put just the letter 'a' into the sha256 hash function, you'll get a large,

bewildering string of digits as an output, but if you did it again
and kept the input exactly the same, just the single letter 'a'
again, you'd get the exact same bewildering output.

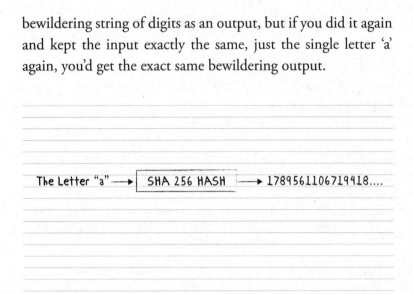

The Letter "a" ⟶ | SHA 256 HASH | ⟶ 1789561106719418....

"This is important because it means anyone using the same
hash function can take your input data and should generate
the same exact output. So in effect, they can check your work.

"Next, the output is totally *unpredictable*. Let's say you ran
the entire dictionary into a hash function and you get a certain
result. Change just one letter, only one letter, in the entire dictionary, for instance, and the resulting hash will be completely
different from the regular dictionary output you just generated, and you would find no correlation whatsoever between
the two.

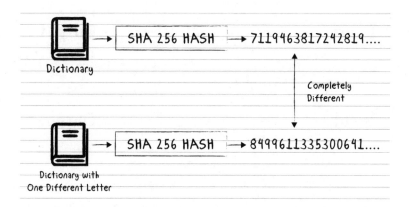

"Are you tracking with me still?"

"I am surprised to say it, but yes, I think I am," said Giulio.

"Great. Next, a hash is *quick and easy* for a computer to run. And further, since the total possible outputs of a 256-bit result is so incredibly huge, it is mathematically very unlikely for any two input strings of data to ever end up with the same result from a hash.

"And here is a very key part: looking at the hash of any particular input of data, it is impossible to arrive back at the original input, meaning a hash is a *one-way function*. You could never generate the input data just by looking at the output data.

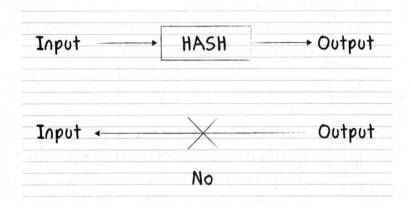

"Still good?"

"Yes, I'm hanging by a thread. Keep going," said Giulio, concentrating.

"Remember, understanding this is worth it. So when I said in my silly accountant analogy that one part of the process of mining is similar to rolling a huge die, here is what I meant. Here is what is actually going on; here's how the race these miners are participating in actually works:

"First, each miner gathers up data for transactions that it finds on the network and makes sure they are valid. This means that they don't violate any of the hard rules written into the program, such as double spending a coin that has already been spent. A miner gathers up and verifies transactions like this until it has enough to fill a block. Then it also grabs the hash of the complete block that was last added to the blockchain. And then, a random number used only once, called a *nonce*, is generated automatically by the Bitcoin program being run by the miner and is attached to this transaction set, and the whole pile of these three inputs is run through the sha256 hash function.

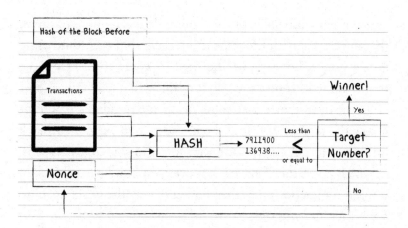

"If the resulting number is *below or equal to* the target number currently set by the Bitcoin program, then that miner wins the race. This computer then announces to the network that it has won and shows its winning output number to the network, along with the input data that it used: the transactions and the hash of the previous block and the nonce. Full nodes throughout the network then verify this by checking that the transactions in the block along with the hash of the last block and also the nonce do in fact hash to what was claimed. They run the hash to check the miner's work. They also confirm that the result of the hash output was lower or equal to the target number, and that the block doesn't have any invalid transactions in it. The work of the winning miner is being checked in this way by all the full nodes in the network. Once all this is verified by the nodes, each node accepts the new block as valid and then writes this new block to its personal copy of the ledger."

"What happens if a miner does all that, runs the hash, and it is larger than the target number?" asked Giulio.

"If the number they get is larger than the target number,

which is what usually happens thousands and millions of times, the miners will hash the same thing again, but each time using a new nonce, hoping that the result is equal to or below the target number. If not, they do it again with a new nonce, over and over until they either come up with a number equal to or below the target number and win the race to write their block onto the blockchain, or until they lose and someone else wins, at which point they have to start over and build a new block of unused transactions that they find and 'play the game' again to see if they can win the next time."

"OK, OK, I think I get it. I really do," said Giulio.

"Good! Then let me throw a term at you that you maybe have heard: *Proof of Work*."

"Yes, I've heard this but I have no idea what it means."

"Well, I've got good news. You actually do now. *Proof of work* is a term that refers to what the miners show when they win a block. Their proof of work is the data they present to the network when they make the claim that they have successfully built a block and won the race. It's the hash result along with the inputs they used to generate that winning hash."

"So they show to the nodes the proof of the work they have done to win."

"You got it. Now, there is something very important about this proof of work concept. Remember how we talked about how it takes super-fast computers that are specially made for the purpose of simply running these hash functions and winning these races?"

"Yes."

"Well, that all comes at an actual cost out in the real world. It requires specialized computer equipment, and the consumption of electricity."

"Yes, that makes sense."

"It costs them something to do it. This provides a barrier against fraudulent actors, because the costs to participate are real. But these costs are worth it to legitimate miners because when they win the race and get to write the new block onto the blockchain, what do they get?"

"Some newly minted bitcoins."

"Yes! So, as the price of bitcoin has gone up over the years, the incentive for miners to win the race has likewise gone up. Therefore, it pays to invest in better and more sophisticated equipment again and again."

"Souping up their race engines to win the prize."

"Right. Especially as the prize has gotten more and more rewarding as the years have gone on and the price of bitcoin out in the open market has gone way up."

"But what sets the price of bitcoin?"

"You mean in terms of dollars or euro?"

"Yes," confirmed Giulio.

"The price of bitcoin, as measured by dollars or euro, is not determined from within the Bitcoin program at all. It is not related to the costs miners must invest in order to play the game and hopefully 'win the race.' The price of bitcoin, rather, is determined in the free market of people who are buying and selling them in exchange for, say, dollars or euro."

"OK."

"So bitcoins are generated inside the program, and all transactions happen inside the network, but the price of bitcoin is determined on the free market by the tug-of-war between buyers and sellers just like the stock price of a company, for instance.

"But let's go back to the race the miners are running. As the competition to win the race intensifies with more and more miners joining the network, it costs more in electricity and more in capital investment in equipment. This real-world cost is another very important feature of the Bitcoin program."

"Why?" asked Giulio.

"Because it makes the issuance of new bitcoins resistant to a *Sybil attack*."

"OK, what's a Sybil attack?" asked Giulio.

"I'll explain with an example. Let's say there is a raffle for a nice car at your local charity."

"Ok. Maybe the Lamborghini Countach we talked about before."

"Perfect, let's stick with that car. It's a really nice one, an expensive classic, but what if the raffle tickets were free? The rule is that everyone can get only one ticket. That keeps it fair. But with such a high prize and no cost required in order to play, do you think it's likely that someone will cheat?"

"Unfortunately, yes."

"And how would they likely cheat?"

"By stuffing the box with a bunch of duplicate tickets to try and increase their odds of winning."

"Exactly. But what happens if, instead of the tickets being free, we suddenly charge $50 for each one that you put into the contest?"

"It would be too costly to stuff the box with duplicate tickets."

"Ok, so this 'stuffing the box with duplicate tickets,' as you say, is what a Sybil attack is. So, since the mining process in

Bitcoin costs something real, in terms of actual costs, as I said before, it prevents someone overwhelming the game with fake blocks. If you want newly minted bitcoins, you're going to have to play the game as specified in the Bitcoin program, which is going to cost you in real-world terms to join this race to try and write the next winning block."

"I can't believe this, Marcus, but I actually think I am kind of understanding this. Lemme ask you something. Is it normal for one's head to hurt at this point?"

"Ha! Yes, probably. But you're catching on quickly."

"I'm not sure I want to admit this, but you're a pretty good teacher. Let's take a break for now. I can't think any more."

Marcus walked upstairs to see if Cassandra was still awake, but her door was shut and it appeared the light inside was off. Marcus glanced at his phone. *How had it gotten so late?* he wondered. His discussion with Giulio had taken much longer than he had anticipated, and he returned to his room aware that Cassandra's emotional account with him had suffered a withdrawal.

15

The next morning Marcus kept his promise to himself and woke up ready to run. The town of Grottaferratta was a fascinating place and very different from anywhere Marcus had ever been. Overhead doors rose, revealing little shops opening for the day's business. Elderly women swept stoops with brooms while old men gathered on benches. Pedestrians scurried along sidewalks, and cars and scooters buzzed through the tiny streets. The sights, sounds, and smells were all new to him, and it occurred to Marcus that there may not be a better way to get acquainted with a foreign city than to jog through its streets.

Returning to the Federici house, he entered the kitchen to find Cassandra unpacking pastries and bread from a paper sack.

"Good morning," she said, smiling.

"Good morning," Marcus answered, giving her a quick kiss on the cheek.

"You and Papa burned the midnight oil last night! How late were you at it?" she asked.

"I'm scared to even tell you."

Cassandra set down a croissant-like cream puff. "How's he

doing with all this Bitcoin stuff?"

"Remarkably well," said Marcus, joining her in her work. "It has helped a lot that he knows so much about finances already, and he is a very intense listener. So I think he's doing very well getting it."

"Why is he so interested? I mean, at first I thought he was just doing it because he knew it was your profession. But based upon the time he is putting in with you on it, I would say he must really be motivated to learn it."

Marcus thought quickly. "Well, I think when I related the plight of the refugees at the Christian House to the problems of government money, and presented Bitcoin as a solution, I think that really got his attention."

"Interesting," said Cassandra. Marcus thought he sensed a note of hesitance in her voice, as if she were not entirely convinced by his reply. Still, she continued in her usual cheery tone. "So today I think I will take you to meet my Nonna, who turned eighty-three two weeks ago. You've been here several days without meeting her, which cannot go on any longer."

"I can't wait," said Marcus.

"You'll love her and she'll love you! She still lives on her own and is the ringleader of all the old widows in her apartment block. She's full of spunk, just like Papa. You'll see where he gets it. The only problem? She speaks not a lick of English. I mean zero, zilch, *nada*."

"Well, I know a good translator," said Marcus.

"Yup, I'm ready. But she speaks very fast! Anyway, after that, Papa is giving a presentation on leadership at a local university. It will be in Italian, of course, but would you like to go and support him? I'd kind of like to hear it and didn't know if you'd mind tagging along."

"Of course."

"Then we've got a plan. Here are some *sfogliatelle*," said Cassandra, handing Marcus two golden-brown triangle shaped pastries with chocolate drizzled on top and nuts sprinkled into the chocolate. "These are my favorite. In America I think they call them lobster tails, but I don't know why. They were originally created in a little town down near Salerno by nuns."

Marcus happily took the platter with its two pastries, sat at the table, spread a napkin on his lap, and took a bite. The crisp outer layer crunched into the soft core of sweet ricotta and candied fruit.

"Um, that's delicious!" he said. "Glad I went on my run this morning!"

"Yeah, I meant to ask you about that. Next time you go running, I go with you, buster!"

"Oops, I'm sorry. I didn't even think to ask!"

"That's OK. You've got a lot on your mind, what with having to make a Bitcoin expert out of Papa and all. Just don't forget that you're here with *me*! And I want to take advantage of every minute together we possibly can!"

"You got it," Marcus answered, and leaned over to give her a sugar-coated kiss.

"Double sweet," she said, kissing him a second time.

Later that evening Giulio and Stefania took Cassandra and Marcus to a seafood restaurant called Fernando Osteria di Pesce, which Cassandra translated as 'Fernando's fish restaurant for locals.' Their entrance was the by-now predictable through-the-kitchen-and-kiss-everyone affair, coupled with many introductions of Marcus, before they finally took their seats at a table that Marcus assumed was their regular place.

"It appeared that the students were very interested in your lecture," Marcus said as they got settled.

"Thank you, yes," answered Giulio, "they were there by choice, not by requirement, so you usually get the cream that rises to the top at such events."

"It sure makes me wish I understood Italian!" said Marcus.

"You should begin studying it," offered Stefania. "You're a smart boy, it would come quickly to you. And I know a good tutor who would be happy to put in the time with you." She smiled, looking in Cassandra's direction.

"What were you covering in the lecture?" Marcus asked.

Giulio sipped some of the before-dinner drink that had been served in a small conical glass and said, "I was actually teaching them about paradigms and confirmation bias and how difficult it is for people to stay open to new ideas. People start to fall backward the moment they think they have something 'figured out.' It has been said, 'Nothing is more securely lodged than the ignorance of the experts.' People learn so much about something that they become narrower and narrower. And some of the biggest problems happen for people when they think they have 'figured God out,'" he said, making air quotes with his hands.

"Papa used Jesus's analogy when he said you can't put new wine into old wine skins," added Cassandra. "He explained that the outwardly spiritual and religious people of Jesus's day wanted what Jesus offered, but they wanted it on their terms; they wanted to mix it into their set religious ways and observances."

"Exactly," chimed in Giulio, "but Jesus was essentially telling them that if they were to accept him, they had to be made new. It was an all-or-nothing deal. And that was very offensive to them, as it is to people of this day. But anyway, I was using that analogy of a complete remaking, a totally new start as a way to illustrate the leadership concept of always learning, always staying hungry, and always being curious—in short, never thinking that you've got something 'figured out,' and that it takes something like a new download of a new program in order to really move forward sometimes and see something new."

"I hate to bring this up, but of course this all reminds me of Bitcoin," said Marcus. "People have to be willing to delete much of what they've been taught about money in order to truly understand Bitcoin and why it matters so much."

"I wondered how long we'd go without Bitcoin making its way into the conversation!" Cassandra said, and Marcus, startled, looked at her closely to gauge her attitude. Was she truly annoyed or just joking? He couldn't be certain either way.

"Well that is right," said Giulio, "with something like Bitcoin, at my age, it is hard to learn. You have to force yourself to be open to new ideas and try to see new paradigms. It is helpful against the aging process, I think, and it can also make life more interesting. Hence my attempt to learn about this Bitcoin stuff."

At that point the server appeared, and as Marcus had come to expect, gave an explanation about each plate placed on the table. Fingers grabbed and forks scraped at food that was all pushed toward Marcus first. "Here, try this Marcus," said Stefania.

"You'll love these ones," said Giulio.

Marcus accepted all the offers hungrily, eying Cassandra

to check her mood. She winked at him and he felt better, but made a mental note to avoid being a 'Johnny One Note.' The last thing he wanted to ever do was become a bore. Still, he had to get Giulio across the threshold of Bitcoin enthusiasm. *Or else, what?* he wondered. Would Giulio really refuse him? These several days had been very smooth, relationally speaking. Marcus sincerely admired Cassandra's parents and enjoyed his time with them, and it seemed that the affection was returned in his direction. But still, Giulio was a strong personality, rightfully protective of his daughter, and Marcus decided he'd better not let the gentility and manners of Giulio, nor his general kindness toward him, lull him into missing the mark. A deal was a deal, and Marcus was more determined than ever to fulfill his part of the bargain.

16

The next morning Marcus returned winded from his run with Cassandra. She had surprised him by setting an aggressive pace, and he was just downing a glass of water when Giulio summoned him to the kitchen table. Cassandra went upstairs to shower as Marcus wiped his brow and grabbed a seat near Giulio.

"Ok, there is a detail I want you to explain to me," Giulio said, paper and pencil ready on the table. "An article I read this morning said Bitcoin is called a *consensus network*. What does that mean?" he asked.

Marcus nodded. "It means that all the nodes have to agree that a newly written block passes a list of rules dictated by the Bitcoin program. There has to be consensus that the latest block meets those rules. If it does, then all the nodes add it to each of their personal copies of the blockchain."

"OK, that's right, you covered that in your analogy with the gym filled with auditors. You said that was what they were doing was verifying that the new blocks met a set of rules," said Giulio.

"Exactly. Each node looks at the proposed new block and, for one thing, makes sure that the amount of newly minted bitcoins dictated in the block matches the current schedule in the Bitcoin program."

"That changes?"

"Yes. There is a schedule that specifies the quantity of new bitcoins awarded for a new block. Over time, the amount given for the winning of a block decreases. But we'll get to that in a minute. The next thing the nodes verify for each transaction inside the proposed new block is that the correct signatures are affixed. These are cryptographic keys that show that the person spending the coins has the right to do so and has authorized the spends. The nodes also look at the proof of work hash of the block and makes sure that it is indeed below the target number. They also make sure the block size is within the size limit as specified in the program. But here's probably the biggest one: the nodes verify that there are no bitcoins being spent in the transactions in this new block that have been spent before. This is where Satoshi solved what is called the 'double spend' problem."

"Its very name describes what it is. But why do I get the feeling that you have more to tell me about it?" asked Giulio.

"You're catching on to my style. Consider when you take a photo on your phone and then say you'll 'send it to me.' Well, you don't really 'send' me that photo, what you essentially do is send me an exact digital duplicate of that photo. Now I have one and you've still got the one you sent me, so we now have two. That's like a double spend. Preventing such a situation presented a puzzle that long eluded cryptographers until Satoshi solved it with the blockchain and mining protocols we've been talking about. The nodes in the Bitcoin network verify that there are no double spends in any of the transactions. In effect, they make sure that if a bitcoin is supposed to move out of your possession and go into my possession, that at the end of that transaction, there is still only one bitcoin in existence. Only now it is mine and not yours. All of this verifying and checking makes this possible. The way it works is that if a double spend is found, the transaction will not be verified, and the new block won't get written onto the blockchain. You may have tried to double spend a bitcoin, but the network won't accept it and it will never be written onto the blockchain. If it doesn't get written onto the blockchain, it doesn't count."

"Genius."

"Absolutely. The breakthroughs represented by the Bitcoin blockchain architecture are staggering when you consider the age-old challenges they solved. There's another brilliant feature in the programming that I especially like, and it's called the *difficulty adjustment*. The Bitcoin software wants to control the pace of the game, meaning it wants new blocks to be written to the code about every ten minutes, not much faster and not much slower. This is important for several reasons. One big one is that the game can't proceed too quickly because there needs to be enough time for a newly winning block to reach all the nodes and get consensus before the next one is put forward. But what if the game goes too slowly? Then what? Well, in that instance it would take a long time for a transaction to become confirmed and users of the network would be inconvenienced, standing around waiting for confirmation of their purchase when they tried to buy something."

"What do you mean for a transaction to be confirmed?"

"Oh, I missed that. Let's go back to the example of you sending me a bitcoin. Once that transaction gets written into a block, it is not 'final' yet. Because in all actuality, in Bitcoin there really is no 'finally,' strictly speaking. There is just layer upon layer of confirmation that would be increasingly impossible to reverse. What I mean is this: once the next block after the one housing our transaction has been written onto the blockchain, that becomes one confirmation that our transaction and our block is being accepted across the whole network. When another block gets written after that, you could then say our transaction has two confirmations. Most people feel pretty comfortable that a transaction is safely confirmed by the time six new blocks have been written after it. The reason is that if someone somehow were able to hack the system and start reversing transactions, it would be increasingly difficult to go back very far. So the more new blocks that are written after the block containing your transaction, the more likely that it is 'final' and will last. I know it's kind of strange, but does that make sense?"

"I suppose so." Giulio leaned back in his chair.

"OK, so how does the Bitcoin program control the speed of the game and average things out so that a new block gets written onto the blockchain about every ten minutes, not faster, and not slower?" Marcus paused so Giulio would have time to let the question sink in, then continued. "Approximately every two weeks, or every 2,016 blocks, to be precise, the program takes a look back to figure out how long it is taking on average to produce those blocks. If it is going too slowly, then that means the game is too hard and the difficulty adjustment needs to make things easier. If the game is going too quickly, it's the opposite, it needs to make things harder. How do you think it could do that?"

"I have no idea at all."

"OK, OK, it's not obvious I suppose, but it is very clever. Remember that target number that all the miners are trying to get below with their hash functions in order to win the next block? Well, the game gets harder if that is a lower number, because there would then be fewer possible numbers that would qualify as being lower than that number. So conversely, it gets easier if the target number is set to a higher number. So every two weeks or so the program looks at the game and adjusts the target number up or down accordingly."

"Wow, that is really amazing. This is a staggering program."

"In many ways it is extremely elegant."

"OK," interrupted Giulio, "but why would the game get faster or slower and need to be regulated?"

"Excellent question! The answer is because the total computational power of all the miners working against each other changes constantly. If a bunch of mining capacity hits the network, the overall hash power, as it is called, goes up. This would make the game go faster. And the opposite is true, of course. Less overall hash power on the network means it will likely take longer to win the races and write new blocks."

"But why would the mining capacity fluctuate like that?"

"There could be many different reasons, but the biggest one seems to be price. When the price of a bitcoin rises in dollar terms, let's say, then it makes more sense for miners to risk their money and spend on equipment and electricity to try and win the game. So overall, the total hash power on the network then goes up. The opposite is true too. Sometimes the volatile price of Bitcoin drops quite a bit and makes mining less worth it. In such cases, many just shut off their mining machines and stop for a while. This decreases the overall hash power on the network."

"Got it."

"But this is another huge reason why the difficulty adjustment is so important. It keeps mining profitable at any bitcoin price."

"Let me think about that," said Giulio. "Yes, I see that. Very clever. Man."

17

Giulio stood, stretched, rubbed his neck, then sat back down and was clearly ready for more. Marcus continued. "OK, there was actually one more reason Satoshi and the original developers wanted to keep the pace of the game at a steady clip, and that has to do with Bitcoin's *monetary policy.*"

"Monetary policy? As in what the central banks do?" asked Giulio.

"Yes! Monetary policy, meaning in this case how the supply of new bitcoins is managed. You see, central banks' monetary policy involves consistently expanding the money supply and thereby devaluing their currencies. Bitcoin, too, has a monetary policy, but quite a different one. And obviously with a very different intent. First of all, Bitcoin is preprogrammed, as I mentioned before, to only have a total of twenty-one million bitcoins ever."

"Yes, I remember that part."

"Further, the rate at which new bitcoins get awarded for the writing of new blocks by miners gets cut in half approximately every four years, or every 210,000 blocks, to be specific. This is called the *halving* of bitcoin. When Bitcoin first launched back in 2009, every new block written onto the blockchain generated a block subsidy of fifty new bitcoins. After about four years, this was cut to twenty-five, then after another four it was cut to 12.5, and currently, it is at 6.25. It will get cut in half again sometime in the year 2024. So today, when a miner wins the race and writes a new block onto the blockchain, it receives 6.25 brand-newly minted bitcoins from the coinbase of the Bitcoin program. Things will continue this way, dropping in half approximately every four years, all the way down until block rewards run out in the year 2140. All of this is what is meant by Bitcoin's monetary policy. It is the preprogrammed plan for how the supply of bitcoins is limited in its total amount, and also how it is metered out over time. It is set, locked, and known. And there is no central person, founder, promoter, authority, group, or council in charge of it that could change it to suit themselves. All of these things, by the way, *cannot* be said of any fiat government currency anywhere in the world. Or for any other cryptocurrency, for that matter. This pre-set, preprogrammed, incorruptible plan for the supply of bitcoins is entirely unique in the whole history of money."

"Again, this is totally genius," said Giulio, spreading his arms as he spoke in a very expressive Italian way. "Incredible, really. A preprogrammed money supply in a world where governments can't keep their finger off their own 'print' buttons. And nobody can mess with this? Its rate is preset?"

"Yes. Preset and basically unchangeable, right in the Bitcoin program. Again, and this is huge, no other cryptocurrency, and certainly no central bank fiat currency anywhere has this factor of immutability. There is a set supply of bitcoin, and an unchangeable plan for how that supply gets rolled out, and that's it. Period. No shenanigans. Truly everything else has a central authority, controller, founder, or interested party of some kind who could at least theoretically mess with the supply. Bitcoin alone is unchangeable. Its known and assured absolute scarcity according to a preset and unmodifiable plan is the biggest factor in the claim for it to be Gold 2.0. Some economists have said that, outside of our own time—meaning the days we have to live—Bitcoin is the thing with a supply most decoupled from demand. It doesn't matter how many more years you want to live—"

"God sets the number of our days," Giulio filled in.

"Right. Doesn't the Bible even say something directly about that?" asked Marcus.

"And which of you by worrying can add a single hour to his life? Jesus said that," interrupted Giulio.

"So the scarcest of commodities in our human experience is our own personal time of life. There is nothing we can do to increase the supply of it, no matter how much we demand it. Next in line is Bitcoin. Its supply is entirely decoupled from its demand. Nothing else is like that. Gold can be mined more aggressively, trillions in dollars or euro of fiat money can be created with just the stroke of a computer key, and all cryptocurrencies except Bitcoin have a person or people who could and often have increased the amount of coins. But Bitcoin is *programmed scarcity*. It is the invention of *absolute scarcity*. This is why it is so important to control the pace of the game, so that new blocks are written about every ten minutes. If it went too fast, it would represent the printing too quickly of new bitcoins, which sounds like—"

"Our friends at the central banks of the world and their politician accomplices printing money like junkies!"

"Yup," nodded Marcus, taking note of Giulio's enthusiasm and calculating that they were indeed making progress toward the goal. "By controlling the pace of the game, the program controls the issuance of new bitcoins, thereby keeping steady control of the monetary policy, and outside the hands of anyone else, even those who would try to speed up the game to make more bitcoins faster."

"I don't know if I have mentioned it to you," said Giulio, "but we Italians have a very low trust of centralized authority. We have lived through so many corruptions and abuses we have become jaded. We've had no lack of scandals around here."

"Are we solving the world's problems?" said Cassandra bounding down the stairs. She joined the two men at the table. Her hair was pulled back in a ponytail, a look Marcus had always appreciated.

Marcus returned her cheery look and Giulio said, "We just might be! We're discussing the world's first decentralized money, one that is out of the reach of scoundrels."

"I should have guessed." Cassandra sighed, looking across the table at Marcus, much of the brightness of her look fading perceptibly.

"Hey, why don't we call it quits for the morning?" asked Marcus.

"Actually, I thought we were just getting warmed up," said Giulio. "You don't mind if we keep going, do you honey?"

Cassandra did mind, as Marcus could clearly read on her face, but she shrugged it off and got up from the table. "OK, just a little while longer, but after that, 'young Marcus' here is mine for the rest of the day. I want to take him to see Abba-

zia San Nilo, and then the Palazzo Apostolico in Castel Gon-
dolfo. Not to mention that he hasn't even had any gelato yet
this whole trip!"

"We haven't had gelato yet? Mamma Mia!" exclaimed Giulio. "What kind of hosts are we?" he kissed Cassandra on the
top of the head. "I promise, I won't keep him too long, honey."

Cassandra slipped from the room and Marcus wished he
were going with her. He was torn between his task and his
target. But Giulio seemed to be orchestrating events at the
moment, so Marcus forced himself to focus on the immediate
objective.

"Believe it or not, we are almost done with the computer
science of Bitcoin," said Marcus. "I mean, there's more, we
could always drill deeper, and there are details and exceptions
and nuances that we could talk about for months, but in terms
of the big stuff, we've gotten through a lot of it. Are you ready
for just a little bit more, though?"

"That's why I shooed my daughter away," said Giulio.

"OK, then here goes. We should discuss the cryptography
aspect."

"Cryptography, as in cyphers and codes?"

"Yes, more or less. And learning this part is important because should you ever decide to get some bitcoin, it will help
you keep it secure.

"OK, with that said, let's begin. In simple terms, cryptography is the study of locks and unlocking those locks. Or said
in a slightly different way, encryption means obscuring some
data so that only someone with the right key can unlock it and
read the original message. Remember, all of this is required
because the system was designed to operate without a trusted

middleman. It has to work between two strangers, on its own. So while what we are about to cover may seem complicated, it's important, because it's one of the main things that makes Bitcoin work," said Marcus.

"Yes," answered Giulio, concentrating.

Marcus continued, "When it comes to Bitcoin, there is something called the *public-private key pair*. Both of these, by the way, the public and the private keys, are 256-bit numbers. Remember those? We learned about them when we talked about the hash function and what miners do."

"Oh yes, how could I forget? The 256-bit numbers were the output of the sha256 hash algorithm. And their biggest feature is that they are incredibly huge," said Giulio.

"Very good! So this is yet another application of 256-bit numbers. As you said, it means that the numbers we are talking about are enormous. The chance of anyone having the exact same string of possibilities in a 256-bit number is nearly impossible. This is useful, because the Bitcoin program generates a 256-bit public key for you, and a corresponding 256-bit private key for you. Both of these, the private and the public keys, are a pair, they work together only, and they are each connected to something called an address. This is arrived at when the Bitcoin program performs a hash of your public key, which will produce a public address. Let me draw this out for you so it will make sense. Just listening to me speak these words has to be confusing, but seeing it drawn out I think will help a lot." Marcus reached for the pencil.

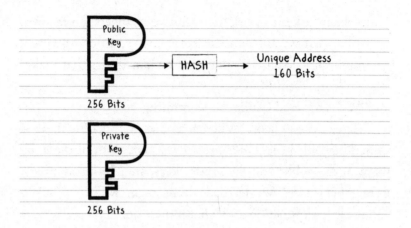

"So as you see here, you are given a Private Key and a Public Key. The program then runs the Public Key through a hash function and produces a unique address. Got it so far?"

"Sure."

"It is important to note that this Public and Private Key are a *pair*, they are hooked together and correspond to that particular address only. The public address is something you can give out to others, so they can use it to send you bitcoins. Then you keep your private key private, because only with that can you access the bitcoins that you might receive in that address."

"Keep the private key private, share the public key and address," said Giulio, with a tone that suggested that this all sounded logical so far.

"You've got it. The best way I know to show this is to use an example. Let's say you are going to send me 1 bitcoin. You would initiate a transaction that looks like this," Marcus said as he drew. "Let's call this the planned transaction, or to keep it simple, we'll just refer to it as the 'message.'"

Address (1984....) containing 1.0 Bitcoins is sending
Giant 160 Bit Number

1.0 Bitcoins to address (5150....)
Giant 160 Bit Number

Planned Transaction or "Message"

"Now, for an analogy. When you use a piece of paper called a personal check to give me some money out of your bank account, you sign your name to the check, thereby authenticating it, right?"

"Yes," said Giulio.

"Well, in similar fashion, when you send me a bitcoin you have to provide a signature authenticating the transaction. You need to prove to the Bitcoin network that you have the private key to this address. But you also don't want to expose your private key to hackers or anybody else. If someone got your private key information, they could use it to unlock what is in this address and move the bitcoins out of there. Your proof of ownership over your private keys is called a *digital signature*. Let me draw it this out for you too," said Marcus.

"Lock" Corresponding
to address (1984....)

Use the Private Key for address (1984....) to encrypt
the "Message" and get a Digital Signature

"Here you can see that what I am calling the message or the planned transaction for this particular address of yours, is then 'locked' or authenticated with your Private Key, and that generates a digital signature. So far so good?"

"Barely." Giulio grimaced.

"Think about it this way," said Marcus. "Your private key is 'locking' the message up by turning it into something called a digital signature.

"Once your message has thus been authenticated with your private key to produce a digital signature, then the next step in the process is that you broadcast to the Bitcoin network three things.

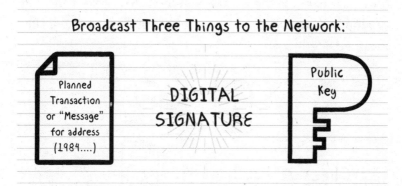

Broadcast Three Things to the Network:

Planned Transaction or "Message" for address (1984....)

DIGITAL SIGNATURE

Public Key

"First, you show the message/planned transaction for this particular address; second, you show the digital signature; and third, you show your public key. Those three things."

"OK."

"Then the network performs two checks on this transaction.

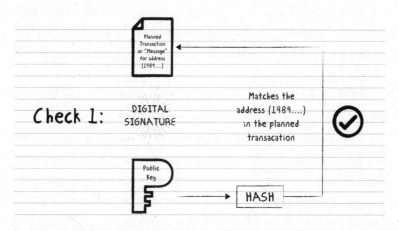

Planned Transaction or "Message" for address (1984....)

Check 1:

DIGITAL SIGNATURE

Matches the address (1984....) in the planned transacation

Public Key

HASH

"The first check is to run the public key you provided through a hash to see if the result of that hash produces an address that matches the address you indicated in your message or proposed transaction. It is just verifying that that public key goes to that address.

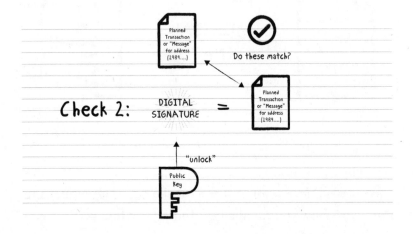

"The second check is to use the public key you provided to unlock the digital signature you also provided which will reveal the message or planned transaction. If this matches the message or planned transaction you provided, then everything checks out."

"OK, I can follow the diagrams, but what is this accomplishing again?" asked Giulio.

"This multi-step process proves that you had the private key for that address. And if you are in possession of the private key for that address, then you are the one who is authorized to initiate a transaction of bitcoins out of that address. Remember that the public and private keys are a pair. The public key can only decrypt messages that were encrypted with the private key. And the network can verify this through the process I just sketched. But importantly, nobody has actually seen your private key but you. So it gave you the authority to initiate this transaction, and allowed no one else that authority. But, through this process, the entire network can verify that you have that authority and no hacker can take it away from you. Does that part make sense?"

"Maybe."

"Let me sketch out the whole flowchart of what is going on here," said Marcus, drawing again.

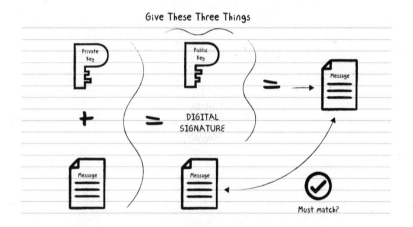

"Ok, I need to keep these drawings to look at. I don't think I can comprehend all this that fast."

"No problem. And it's important to understand that addresses are only used once. The best way to think of them is as a 'one-time lock.'"

"OK."

Suddenly Cassandra approached. "You fellas at a stopping point?" she asked.

"Um, I'm sorry, but can I just explain one more thing to your dad?" Marcus asked, knowing he risked annoying her.

But, he reasoned to himself, he had a bit more to teach Giulio about the cryptography of Bitcoin or he might have to start all over.

"OK, then," said Cassandra. "Just come get me when you are done. I'll be upstairs."

Giulio didn't seem to notice his daughter's mood, but Marcus could actually feel it.

"What's the one more thing?" asked Giulio.

18

I was hoping that one more analogy might help complete the picture for you regarding these public and private keys," said Marcus.

"OK, shoot," answered Giulio.

"Imagine this. Right in the main piazza of Grottaferratta there is a big long set of lockers, like what you might find inside a school."

"Lockers, OK."

"So let that long row of lockers be the Bitcoin network. Picture thousands and thousands of lockers."

"Got it."

"And every single locker has the exact same kind of lock on it. A very special type of two-key lock. One key locks it, and the other key unlocks it. No key will unlock it unless it has been locked first.

"Also each locker has a specific serial number on it, which we can say is its address. Let's say you are assigned a new locker by the Bitcoin network and you have some bitcoins in it. You go there so you can send me the one bitcoin we used in our example. You have two keys, the private key and the public key. They only work on that one locker with a particular address.

Follow?"

"Yes. Sure."

"So you go to the piazza, you look at this enormous, long assembly of lockers, and you find your specific locker, the one with your address on it. You write a note that you want to move one of the bitcoins in there over to me, and you do that by putting my locker number, or my address, on that piece of paper. Then you put that paper inside the locker, and you lock it using the private key. You then give a copy of the public key to everyone on the network, and they all use it to open the lockbox and find out that yes, the public key you gave them did indeed open that lock, which would not have opened unless it had been locked first with your private key. This proves to them that you had the authority to do it, so they read what is on the paper to see your intentions for this transaction, verify that there is a bitcoin in there, and agree that you can move that bitcoin from your locker into mine. This is one of the things that the miners are doing when they gather up transactions and verify them. They check out this private key authorization by going through the steps we have been describing.

"I gave you this clunky analogy because I want to explain something called *wallets*. The term is a little bit unfortunate, because when we think of wallets we think of billfolds, which are just that: a place where we fold up paper bills and keep them safe. But with Bitcoin, a wallet doesn't actually hold any money. It doesn't hold any bitcoins. It actually simply holds your private keys. So it might be more accurate to say, instead of a wallet, that you have a Bitcoin *key ring*."

"OK," said Giulio. "How do you use a wallet?"

"A wallet is the place where you keep track of your private

keys. Continuing with the locker analogy, let's say that you've got some bitcoins. To access them, you walk to the assortment of lockers in the piazza and use your private keys to access a particular locker at a particular address. The thing you carried the private keys in as you made your way to the lockers was called a wallet. It doesn't have bitcoin in it, just the keys to your particular addresses. The bitcoins stay in the network, in the big long line of lockers, all the time. Bitcoins never leave that huge set of lockers. They just move around between lockers based upon the instructions those with public/private key pairs give. So no bitcoins in the wallet. It's the keys that you store safely in a wallet."

"I think I've got the distinction."

"That's why the analogy of the lockers. That huge bank of lockers represents the Bitcoin network. I wanted you to picture yourself going there, fumbling with your keys, and using them to access the bitcoins in your locker. No keys, no access. Period. And, even with the keys, you don't ever get to take your bitcoins out of that long line of lockers, you can only keep them in your particular lockers or pass them to others within that system of lockers. That's it. Got it?"

"Yes. So wallets are the key, no pun intended," said Giulio.

"Ha, yes, that's a good one! And it's totally correct. Wallets are the key. I'm going to use that! OK, so, there are different types of wallets. *Hot wallets* are software wallets that are connected to the internet in some way, either through a desktop or laptop computer, or a mobile device. *Cold wallets* are mechanical devices that are not connected to the internet and are therefore not hackable. You plug them into the internet in order to get your private keys from the Bitcoin network, then you disconnect them and place them somewhere safe. Another type of cold wallet is simply a piece of paper with your keys printed out on it—totally safe from hackers, but also easy to lose or inadvertently destroy. Remember, wallets do not store your bitcoins, they only store your private keys which you need to go to the network and access your bitcoins. Is this making sense?"

"Yes, I think so, but this last hour is all pretty fuzzy."

Giulio asked to review some of the diagrams Marcus had sketched and asked many questions. Marcus answered each one carefully but was beginning to feel uncomfortable with the growing resentment he sensed coming from Cassandra. While encouraged by his progress with Giulio so far, he knew he needed to spend some time with the woman he had come all the way to Italy to woo. He ached to tell her what was going on, but he reminded himself how much she liked surprises and he hung onto the image in his mind of how perfect it would be to propose to her at the end of his stay.

For his part, Giulio was inquisitive, smart, and expending a lot of energy to understand Bitcoin. Marcus was pleasantly surprised with Giulio's ability to comprehend new concepts and also his knowledge of money and broader disciplines. Giulio hadn't lived a full life of over fifty-odd years for nothing. Marcus admired him and hoped he would be as eager to learn new things when he hit that age. But as the minutes dragged on, Marcus was convinced he needed to attend to the needs of a certain dark-haired beauty. Just as he was about to excuse himself, Giulio asked a question that would take some serious time to address properly.

"OK young Marcus, you have taken me on quite a tour of Bitcoin's computer science, and though I can't say I understand it all, I do feel as if I've got the grasp of the general concept and how Bitcoin goes about its business. I will certainly have more questions. But can you explain to me how it went from being a computer science experiment in the hands of a small group of geeks, to a super valuable thing out in the real world? I can't figure out how it leapt from a computer program running on a few computers to something that is worth real money paid by real people."

Marcus glanced up and to the left and thought for a moment. "I tell you what, can you excuse me for just a second? I have an idea."

Giulio shrugged and nodded. In seconds Marcus was out the kitchen door and striding across the back patio, headed for the olive trees, his cell phone to his ear.

"Ari, it's Marcus."

"Hey Marcus, how goes the crisis? Is the old man a Bitcoiner yet?"

"Well, no, not really, but I'll tell ya, we've made great progress."

"Did all that stuff I sent help?"

"Yeah, especially that first night when we mostly talked about economics and the reason why Bitcoin was invented," answered Marcus.

"Great. Let me know if you need any more of that kind of stuff, I've got tons of it."

"Well, that's kinda why I'm calling."

"Shoot."

"You see, I'm doing a balancing act over here. I came all the way to Italy to spend time with Cassandra and ask her to marry me. But right now, she's probably thinking I'm more interested in marrying her dad!"

"Ha! What would make her think that?"

"Because I'm spending so dang much time teaching him about Bitcoin. And she can't know what I'm up to or why I'm suddenly so committed to this Bitcoin-for-boomers school I'm running over here."

Ari laughed. "Dude, you're in a tight spot."

"Yeah, but here's how you can help me. Right now!"

"OK, OK, I promised I would help. What can I do?" asked Ari, getting serious.

"Giulio, that's her dad's name."

"Yeah, I think you told me that last time when you called."

"OK, sorry, I can't remember. I'm getting a little stressed. Anyway, Giulio and I have been talking all morning and I've got to go spend some time with Cassandra. But he just asked a really good question and he expects me to answer it right now, I think."

"And?" asked Ari.

"I would like to put you on the phone with him and let you answer it while I sneak away and patch things up with Cassandra."

"Me? Right now?"

"Yeah, man, come on, be a friend. Hook a brother up."

"Aw, uh, OK, I said I would help. But I've got people coming in the door right now. Are you sure you can't arrange it for tomorrow or something? I'd be glad to help, but I can't just back out of hosting this party right now."

"Come on! You can do it! Maybe it won't take that long, I don't know," pleaded Marcus.

"Hold it, what's the question?"

"It's actually a really good one. One I don't think I've ever been asked before. He wants to know how Bitcoin went from being a computer program shared among a small group of computer nerds to escaping into the real world and having a real price, and a real use, and being used to pay for real things. In other words, how did it jump from concept to reality and become so big?"

"Wow."

"I told you he was a smart guy."

"Yeah, that's a super good question," said Ari, a more hopeful tone in his voice. "And you know what? I think I have a way out of both of our dilemmas."

"How's that?" asked Marcus.

"Katya."

"Of course!" cried Marcus.

"Yeah, she's the expert on Bitcoin history, has written loads of articles on that very subject, and I guarantee you she could do a better job of it than either you or me, or both of us put together, for that matter."

"Great idea! Can you get her to do it right now, though?"

"Probably, she just walked in the door!"

"Yes, but in party mode."

"No, dude, she'll do it. She owes me big time."

"OK, fantastic. I'll text you Giulio's number and she can video chat with him. I think that'd be best."

"I'm on it. Stand by for confirmation by text," said Ari signing off.

Marcus returned to the kitchen table where Giulio had poured them each a glass of sparkling water, apparently ready to settle into learning the answer to his question. But Marcus

was quick to share the new plan, assuring him that Katya Iwan-
icki was by far the best person to answer his question. Giulio,
much to Marcus's relief, was open to it and said he would eagerly await her call. Thus free to roam, Marcus bounded up the
stairs to rescue his damsel in distress.

19

Cassandra and Marcus sat on a park bench near a fountain on a busy corner in Frascati, enjoying gelato and tasting each other's flavors. The mid-afternoon sun was strong as they sat close and talked about nothing and everything at once. People of all sorts rushed by in random directions and the cacophony of horns and Vespas provided a soundtrack of endearing chaos.

"So what is up with you and my dad spending so much time together?" asked Cassandra. "Don't get me wrong, I'm super glad you're hitting it off so well, but I thought you came to Italy to see *me!*" Her tone was gentle and even playful, but Marcus knew the question was real. He was amazed at this cosmopolitan woman who could switch from the dutiful Italian daughter who always kissed her dad first and called him 'Papa,' but then later alone with Marcus would often refer to Giulio like an American as 'my dad.' Even as he had this thought of wonder and admiration for her, he realized he needed to answer carefully.

"No one is more surprised by it than me!" said Marcus. "I flew over here almost fearful of the guy, hoping beyond hope that I'd make a good impression on him. And then I discover he can't get enough of learning about my profession. I'll tell you this, though, he is a very smart guy, which makes this teaching of Bitcoin to him actually easy, and enjoyable."

Cassandra smiled. "I find it funny you were afraid of him! He's a teddy bear. But I understand why."

"Uh, yeah? If he didn't approve of me, how long would you have stayed in love with me?"

"First of all, my love for you is not contingent upon my father's view of things, no matter how old-fashioned and close-knit my family is. Second, there was no way he *wouldn't* approve of you."

Marcus smiled. "Thank you for saying that, but there was no way I could have known that coming in. I also think I might have underestimated him. I don't know, maybe I assumed a stereotype for him."

Cassandra nodded, finishing a bite of Straciatella gelato. "I don't buy into the stereotypes of Christian preachers at all," she said, swallowing. "But if I did, my dad certainly shatters most of them. He has lived a life around all kinds of people, from those who wonder where their next meal is coming from, on one hand, to celebrities and high-profile public figures on the other. He knows a lot about a lot, has always been an avid reader, and somehow always wants to learn more."

"I see that. That's how I want to be when I'm his age. He seems so young, too. I think it's his native curiosity and his desire to learn. It's been amazing, really, getting him up to speed on Bitcoin, especially the economics. He already had a grasp of what is broken with the world's money, which is more than I could say for most people I talk to. When explaining Bitcoin, you have to first define the problem, which some people just can't or won't see. It seems as if many people just blindly accept things the way they are, trust whatever their government or the elite tells them, and follow like sheep. But your dad, he thinks for himself," Marcus said.

"He's a rascal, as he likes to say. For him the term doesn't have a negative connotation, but instead means someone who follows his own convictions and stands on principle, even if the crowd is going the other way. He likes to say, 'one has to start with first principles and work up from there.' It is a deliberate approach to life, and it requires courage."

"That's a good model for us all," nodded Marcus.

"Yes, I think so too. One of the things he is always teaching is that you have to beware when you think you have something 'figured out.' He uses that to describe God, first, and how people become doctrinaire and dogmatic when they think they have figured out God. God has revealed himself to us in the Bible, but he is infinite and will never be fully comprehended and 'figured out' by us mere mortals. I guess you heard him talk about that a little at the university. But this warning applies to everything. He talks about the top of the learning curve as a peak that can actually turn back downward, meaning, there can be a point in learning more and more that leads to less and less effectiveness. He warns that sometimes more learning on a topic makes one narrower, not better. And eventually, all that learning makes one think he is an expert, to the point where new inputs coming in are all seen to confirm the conclusions that the expert has already drawn up for himself. Everything feeds the expert's confirmation bias. Everything that doesn't fit gets rejected as incorrect. So the danger in much learning is narrowness. While conversely, the danger in ignorance is shallowness."

"That's deep," said Marcus.

"This is serious!"

"I know, I'm sincere. Oh, ha! I didn't even notice the pun. No, but that is good what you just said. I should be Tweeting all of this!" Marcus downed the last scoop of his gelato.

"So vanilla," Cassandra said, watching him throw his cup away in an adjacent bin.

"Yup. It's always been my favorite. It's the one true flavor. All others are mere modifications of the original."

"Sounds pretty narrow."

Marcus laughed. "Ouch, I guess you're right!"

"But you liked my Straciatella, didn't you?" Cassandra asked.

"I like your everything, even if I can't pronounce it." He kissed her gently. His desire for her was strong and it made him think of his larger objective while here in Italy, which took his thoughts back to Giulio and how he might be progressing with Katya at the moment.

"What are you thinking about?" asked Cassandra, noticing the far-away look in his eyes.

"Nothing. Just building castles in the sky," he said and kissed her again.

"Well, speaking of castles, we should probably get going. I want to show you the Villa Aldobrandini. You'll love the architecture, as you always do, but wait till you see the views from up there. It feels like you can see eternity."

"By all means, lead the way," Marcus said with a comical bow of gentility, attempting to sound like Lin-Manuel Miranda in *Hamilton*. And as they walked, hand-in-hand, Marcus allowed himself a moment of excitement that quite possibly, in a week's time, he and this lovely woman would be engaged to be married. He was already seeing eternity, or at least 'til death do us part.'

20

Meanwhile, back at the Federici home, Giulio had moved out onto the back patio in a shaded area and settled into a lounge chair, holding his phone up in front of his face and conversing loudly with the young woman on the screen who was a quarter-of-a-world away.

"So, where are you from?" asked Giulio.

"I was born in Ukraine but moved to the States with my parents when I was twelve," answered Katya.

"And now you are a Bitcoin journalist?"

"Well, that is a little bit too formal sounding, but yes, one of my passions is capturing the history of the development of Bitcoin and teaching people about it. Marcus and Ari's company sponsors some of my work."

"Ah, OK. Well, so do you understand my question?" asked Giulio.

"I think so. You want to know how Bitcoin went from a little tiny computer experiment to something that is out in the real world that has actual value. Have I got it right?"

"Yes."

"Well, that's a very good question, and frankly, one that isn't often taught when people are trying to explain Bitcoin to someone new. It's not really even captured in the books that teach Bitcoin to beginners. But I think I can help you out. How much has Marcus told you? Has he explained Bitcoin mining and proof of work, for instance?"

"Yes, but don't test me on them," answered Giulio.

"OK, well let's start there. Since I don't know exactly what he's told you, there may be some repetition here, but maybe that will help anyway. Here goes. Did Marcus mention something called the Byzantine Generals Problem?"

"Um, no."

"OK. It's an allegory used to describe a computer science problem, specifically the problem of constructing a truly decentralized network, what we call a 'trustless' system."

"Yes, Marcus has talked to me about trustless."

"OK, good. Picture a fortified city that a bunch of Byzantine military generals have surrounded. To make a successful assault, all the generals and their troops must attack at the same time. But to coordinate such an attack, the messages passed between the generals need to be accurate and trustworthy. But such a system would be open to many points of failure. The messengers could be traitorous. One or more of the generals could be traitorous and issue retreat orders instead. Messengers could be kidnapped and compromised. You get the idea."

"Yes," answered Giulio.

"So for computers to truly come up with a decentralized system, akin to a bunch of generals surrounding a city and needing to coordinate an attack, such a system would need a way to still function properly even if some of the participants were traitors. In any proposed decentralized money system, the biggest specific type of faulty behavior would be something called a *double spend*. Did Marcus discuss with you the double spend problem?"

"Yes, he did."

"OK, so the solution to this Byzantine generals problem and the specific problem of double spending, is something called the *Byzantine fault tolerance algorithm*. It is a computer program that features a *consensus mechanism*. This seeks as much agreement from the participants as possible, incentivizes the participants to collaborate for the good of the group, gives equal weight to the vote of each participant, and gets as many of the participants involved as possible to represent the true majority. These are the principles that the inventor of Bitcoin, Satoshi Nakamoto, had to embody in his solution. OK?"

"Yes."

"So Satoshi's solution to the Byzantine Generals Problem and specifically the double spend, was a special class of consensus mechanisms called the *Nakamoto Consensus*. This works on the principle that the nodes in the network need to have 'skin in the game' in order to incentivize their honest participation in the system. Any successful money must be difficult to create. Its creation must be costly so it can't be easily counterfeited. This is called *unforgeable costliness*. The way Satoshi engineered this to work with Bitcoin is called *proof of work*, and is what Bitcoin miners do. Did Marcus explain proof of work and mining?"

"Yes, but again, I'm only understanding it at a basic level," answered Giulio.

"That's OK. The key thing to know about miners is that they have to spend real-life resources in order to participate in this game of winning bitcoins. The process of procuring the winning hash in the mining process is difficult and costly, but (and this is important) checking the validity of the winning solution put forward by miners is easy for the nodes across the network to do. So mining is hard and costly, but checking their work is cheap and easy. If I've lost you with all this terminology, just know this: the system is hard to cheat because it costs something to participate in, but the results are easily checkable. If a messenger tried to show up with a false message, the work is easy to check, so the nodes would reject it. That's the concept."

"OK."

"So individual actors can't go astray without spending real world resources in order to do so, and even if they do, they simply get ignored by the system. Further, the overall system would be very hard to attack because it would require 51 percent of the network's hash power to do so, and that would be exceedingly expensive to accomplish, and unimaginable to coordinate. So, the miners are doing two things. First, they are *verifying transactions* and writing the record, meaning, they are assembling the blockchain of proper transactions. And second, they are *securing the network* by contributing all of their hash power. So, the more miners and the higher the hash power, the more secure the network against attack. This is one of the big contributing factors to the overall high security of the Bitcoin network. Its overall hash power is staggeringly high.

"It is these inventions—the block chain as a public ledger, miners as writers of new blocks and verifiers of transactions, nodes who only accept blocks that satisfy the rules, and proof of work as a cost to participate and a barrier against cheating— that represent the solution to the problems that had always prevented a decentralized system. These are the breakthroughs that made it all possible. Are you following me at all?" asked Katya.

"Well, Marcus covered some of this with me before, so yes, I think I am tracking, at least in an overall sense. But I must say, the way you summarized it just then helped me gain more clarity."

"OK, great. That's all that's important, just getting it from a conceptual standpoint. And that's the reason I am reviewing this with you, because in all of this is the answer to your question. In the early days of Bitcoin, you had a small group of interested individuals who were running the Bitcoin program on their computers and chatting and emailing back and forth about it. That's it. There were many bugs in the program, and typical to an open source project, the various cypherpunks, as they called themselves, each pitched in and proposed solutions and code to try and make the program better and better. Satoshi then did something pretty important: he launched the Bitcoin forums. This was a gathering place where all interested people could join and freely and easily discuss the development of Bitcoin. This was when the numbers of people interested in this project grew exponentially."

"And why did people get interested?" asked Giulio. "What was the attraction?"

"A very good question," replied Katya. "At first, it was this little circle of computer geniuses who enjoyed cryptography and the challenge of inventing a decentralized system. That's the cypherpunks I mentioned. A group of them had been working on this stuff dating back at least a couple decades, believe it or not. They were trying to use cryptography to secure freedom and privacy for individuals. And there had even been multiple attempts at decentralized money which, of course, all failed. But as the major issues were solved and the Bitcoin program was made better and better, word spread to the wider software development world and more programmers got involved. These programmers were motivated by the same thing that motivated Satoshi: the idea of a system of currency that wasn't controlled by government or central bankers. The truth is that Bitcoin was developed by many very capable people.

"But don't get the idea that this was a harmonious, happy group. Open-source projects are never like that. They are contentious and prickly, as each person is there with his or her own opinions, each fighting to be heard, each trying to win consensus approval for the direction of the project and the implementation of some of their code fixes. And these are volunteers, super capable ones at that. They don't have to be there. They have no boss or authority over them."

"They're a bunch of rascals! Bitcoin was built by rascals," quipped Giulio, as much to himself as to Katya. "Amazing."

"Well, yes, really, they were. We could use terms ranging from 'disrupters' to 'revolutionaries' to describe them, I suppose. But overall this jumble of strong individuals working together in a seemingly anarchic fashion was a very productive order-out-of-chaos thing. And that's what happened in the early days of Bitcoin."

"So this Satoshi Nakamoto character wasn't the boss?" asked Giulio.

"Yes and no. In the early days he was just another one of the very few participants, many of which were all using pseudonyms, which is the norm, anyway. And amazingly, for a period of time there, absolutely nothing happened! I mean, here you invent decentralized money, for Pete's sake, and nobody cares! It reminds me of that quote that goes something like, 'don't worry about anyone stealing your good idea. If your idea is any good, you'll have to—'"

"Cram it down people's throats!" interrupted Giulio.

Katya laughed. "Yes, that's it. There were actually periods of time in 2009 when weeks would go by and there wouldn't be any transactions on the Bitcoin network at all. Zero. It's hard to believe now, but it's true. I mean, imagine you have invented something so world-changing, and yet you have to then actually promote it to others! That's what Satoshi had to do. But then, eventually, people started realizing the elegance of Satoshi's solutions to the main problems decentralized systems had always faced. As that happened, he was treated pretty reverently for a while. But then the project got so big, the participants grew in number to be so large, that the whole thing kind of outgrew any central person.

"Ultimately, Satoshi had to solve the riddle of himself. How could there be a central guiding figure to a decentralized system? I mean, he invented decentralized money! This very well might be the biggest invention of our lifetimes. How could he not be seen as an authority? And in the early days, people were emailing him and asking him on chat about this or that question. Lots of people seeking his input. But there were also others who began to question his authority and push back on any central influence of any kind. Then in late 2010, he simply disappeared. And that was how he put the final piece of decentralization into place. That was well over ten years ago and the project has only moved forward, leaderless. It's truly incredible."

"OK, I am picturing this scene. But how did it connect to the real world?"

"Well, this is why I reviewed the mining process and proof of work with you. Like I said, it is important that you understand that part at least conceptually, because it is the fact that mining has a real-world cost that 'seeded' Bitcoin into the real world. As more and more people got involved, the overall hash rate of the network went higher and higher. This meant that it was costing more and more to win bitcoins. So at first, real world costs equaled real world value. And the early participants started talking about this. They wondered what a bitcoin was worth. At the very least, it should be worth what it had cost to mine, they thought. But they of course wondered if it could be used to buy actual things out in the real world, and how that would be done. Then along came something called an *exchange*. Has Marcus told you about those yet?"

"No, not yet."

"Picture an exchange like an on-ramp to an expressway. If the Bitcoin network was the expressway, exchanges became the way you connect real money to it. Let's say you wanted to get some bitcoins back in those early days. There were only two ways to get them. One: you learn to run the Bitcoin software program, do some mining, and earn some bitcoins that way. In the early days when the hash power was very low because there were few participants, it was that easy. This quickly changed, of course. The second way to get bitcoins would have been to find someone who had some on the network, then hand them some cash in exchange for them sending you bitcoins on the network to your address. That was it."

"OK, got it."

"But there needed to be a more convenient way more accessible to more people, and that's where exchanges came in. An exchange is a company that allows you to put in dollars or euro or whatever, and 'exchange' them for bitcoins. In effect, the exchanges act a lot like a stock brokerage account. You set up an account with them, connect it to your bank, deposit some money, and then whenever you want you can buy some bitcoins with your money. The exchanges would either give you your own digital wallet to hold your bitcoin keys, or they would just hold onto the bitcoins for you. This latter option is called *custody*. The exchanges were often custodians for most of their customers who had bought bitcoins through them. The customers didn't hold their own keys to their own bitcoins, the exchanges just held a bunch of bitcoins on behalf of their customers. This turned out to be a problem, because there were some famous hacks of these early exchanges and people lost their bitcoins."

"I thought Bitcoin has never been hacked?" asked Giulio.

"The Bitcoin network never has. But these early exchanges weren't very sophisticated, and some of them were famously hacked. Today, exchanges have come a long way, and there are some massive ones and even publicly traded ones, meaning, you can own stock in them on the stock market. They are much safer today than back in the beginning. But still, it is a good idea when you buy bitcoins on an exchange—which is how almost everybody, from individual investors to professionals, does it nowadays—to use a wallet and keep control of your private keys yourself. Move them off of the exchange and take custody of the keys yourself. One of the sayings of hardcore Bitcoiners is, 'no keys, no coins,' meaning, if you don't hold your private keys in your own custody, you don't really have complete possession of your bitcoins."

"Marcus taught me about public and private keys and wallets," said Giulio.

"OK, good. I'm sorry it is taking so long to answer your question, but I promise, I am answering it in stages. At the end, you will see how it all came together. But first, we have to talk about pizza."

"Pizza?" asked Giulio, wondering where this conversation could possibly go next.

21

Yes, pizza," said Katya. "Remember how I said that at an early point in the development of Bitcoin, the only value the participants could agree on for bitcoins was, at the lowest level, the cost required to mine them?"

"Yes," answered Giulio.

"Well, it wasn't long before they began wondering what they could buy in the real world. On May 22, 2010, a day that will forever after be referred to as 'Pizza Day' in Bitcoin folklore, a Bitcoin enthusiast in the United States named Laszlo Hanyecz decided to try an experiment. He went on a Bitcoin talk forum and said that he would pay 10,000 bitcoins to anyone who would deliver to him two large pizzas. He said he didn't care if the person made it himself or ordered it from a local pizza joint. Interestingly, a man in England took him up on his offer and made a phone call to the Papa John's pizza shop located near Hanyecz. Two large pizzas were delivered, and Hanyecz then transferred 10,000 bitcoins across the Bitcoin network to the sender of the pizzas."

"A real-world application," said Giulio, "but an astronomically good deal for the sender now! My goodness, what would 10,000 bitcoins be worth today?" asked Giulio.

"According to today's bitcoin price, it would be hundreds of millions of dollars!"

"Oh man! That must hurt for the guy who bought the pizza!" said Giulio.

"That's what everybody thinks, but actually, Hanyecz has been interviewed about it and he has a pretty good attitude regarding the whole thing. He reminds everyone that they really had no idea how to value bitcoins back in those days, and it was a pretty cool early effort to find out if they could actually be spent for something real."

"Yeah, I get it."

"In those early days, too, there were some misconceptions about bitcoins. People thought that using them was anonymous, which isn't strictly true. Given a starting point and just a little information, experts are able to do the forensics and trace purchases back to addresses. If any information about those addresses is made public, the anonymity goes away. Satoshi's idea of anonymity was meant to serve the trustless system, not to shield people's actions entirely. But this early misinterpretation led to another type of early adopter of Bitcoin."

"The bad guys," Giulio interrupted.

"Yes. People began using bitcoins to pay for illegal things. Again, this happened because they thought it was anonymous. The most high-profile development of this was something called the Silk Road. It took its name from the ancient trade route across Central Asia that brought goods to the Middle East and later the Roman Empire. And it was a website that sold drugs, guns, prostitution services, and pretty much anything illegal you can think of. There is no doubt that nefarious uses for Bitcoin like this made some amount of contribution to its early 'seeding' into the real world. This was an early and persistent application of the use of bitcoins to buy real things."

Giulio nodded. "I once read how the early days of the internet were similarly seeded by the popularity of chat rooms and people who would go in there under anonymous names and talk dirty to each other. It's unfortunately inherent in human nature for sin to find ways of exploiting any new technologies." Giulio was a student who was also always ready to teach.

"I guess that is an exact parallel. I never thought of that before, but I can clearly see it. So yes, Silk Road and that type of thing had a part to play in the early connection of Bitcoin to real world purchases. But there was another attraction, and that was price action."

"Yes?"

"Yes. As more and more people got involved in Bitcoin, and as more and more money was transferred to buy it on exchanges, and as there were increasing uses of it to purchase actual things, illicit or otherwise, there started to be a pretty traceable price for it. And, just as would happen with anything in a free market, if the price goes up enough, and quickly enough, that alone is going to attract attention," explained Katya.

"So speculators came in," said Giulio.

"Yep. The lure of easy profits brought in the speculators, whose actions of course drove the price up, too. The more the price went up, the more 'money' people made off of their investment in Bitcoin, and the more others wanted to participate. It was a giant FOMO. Do you know FOMO?"

"Yes. Fear Of Missing Out," answered Giulio.

"So that led to the need for more exchanges, which made it easier for more people to buy bitcoins, which drove the price up higher still. Then, some of the early Bitcoiners began setting up companies that would allow people to spend their bitcoins at actual stores. The stores didn't have to understand the technology or actually receive bitcoins at all, these companies would take care of all of that at the point of purchase. A customer could show up, pay in bitcoins, and these services would take the bitcoins for themselves and give the merchant the equivalent in their local currency. This was a rapidly growing sector of Bitcoin for a while."

"What happened?"

"Well, gradually, the mass of people buying into Bitcoin were doing so as an investment, and the whole 'Gold 2.0' narrative started to win the day. The use of Bitcoin as a medium of exchange, meaning, spending it to buy things, didn't make that much sense because the value of it was going up so steeply."

"Nobody wanted to be the next pizza guy, you mean," said Giulio.

"Yes, that's exactly right. Then the US government declared that Bitcoin was a commodity and should be taxed as such. This was an important inflection point because it then meant that if you bought bitcoins and then later spent them, if they had gone up in value, you now owed a capital gains tax on the difference. Not only did this make the spending of bitcoins expensive, but it also made it complicated and cumbersome. Who wants to track their tax burden every time they buy a coffee?"

"Ouch."

"Yes, so the increasingly investable nature of Bitcoin as an asset on one side, and its tax requirements on the other, combined to cool off the use of Bitcoin as a medium of exchange.

There are multiple phases to the adoption of a money by society, anyway. The first one is simply as a curiosity or collectible. Bitcoin was certainly that in its early days. The next one is as a store of value and a speculative bet, because its value is seen to be going up. The phases after that involve it being used as a medium of exchange, and because of the reasons I've just outlined, Bitcoin never fully crossed into that third category. Though, don't get me wrong, you can more easily spend Bitcoin today than ever before. And I don't know if Marcus has talked about this yet or not, but sending bitcoins around the world in any amount is easier than with any other form of money or payment system."

"Yes, but again, nobody wants to become the pizza guy."

"I suppose. But even so, there is a market in Bitcoin for people who send remittances abroad. It is much easier to send bitcoins than fiat currency, say, if you are an immigrant working in the US to support your family back home in an undeveloped country somewhere. Conventional methods are expensive, cumbersome, and often dangerous. Not so with Bitcoin. It's easy, affordable, and open to anyone anywhere at any time."

"Freedom money, Marcus has said," said Giulio.

"Precisely," answered Katya. "Hey, a final thing we should discuss is something called Metcalfe's Law. Have you ever heard of it?"

"I'm not sure," answered Giulio.

"It is a simple formula that essentially says that a network gets more valuable with each new node that gets added to that network. Specifically it says that the value of a network equals the number of nodes in that network, squared. For instance, if you had the only cell phone in the world, it wouldn't be that valuable. But as soon as someone else gets a cell phone, the value of your phone goes up because now you at least have someone to call. As more and more people get cell phones, the value of cell phones and the ability to call anyone in the network goes up. In this way, value increases.

"I think this is the final thing to think about when trying to understand how Bitcoin went from being small and insignificant to huge and valuable; its network grew to be enormous. It fulfilled Metcalfe's Law. Bitcoin literally spans the world. There are tens of thousands of active Bitcoin nodes that we know of, not to mention the untold number that exist behind firewalls and are otherwise obscured from being countable. Essentially, Bitcoin holds a near monopoly on the idea of programmable money. There are thousands of copycats, but as I'm sure Marcus will explain to you, truly none of them offer what Bitcoin does, although one or two are interesting to be sure. But the point is that Bitcoin has stood the test of time, gotten to a market cap of over $1 trillion and continues to grow. The very fact that it was able to get this big in a little over a decade is so indescribably incredible that I have trouble formulating words to express it.

"Well, anyway, I should probably be getting back to this party. But did I answer your question at all about how Bitcoin got connected to society? I tried to provide the wide sweep of events that made it happen."

"Yes, young lady, you did a great job. Thank you for your time. Now please go join your friends at that party," said Giulio, easily slipping into the fatherly role.

"OK, will do, and nice meeting you! Tell Cassandra I said hi!"

22

That evening Cassandra and Marcus returned to the Federici home in the best of moods. Their day together, after a sputtering start, had been dream-perfect. Now Cassandra was teasing Marcus about his dog phobia. The two were laughing uncontrollably as they entered the house, putting smiles on the faces of Stefania and Giulio who were seated at the kitchen table.

"What are you two kids up to now?" asked Stefania, dressed smartly as ever.

"Oh! Marcus and his lack of understanding of the canine world!" laughed Cassandra.

Right on cue, little Crescendo raced into the room and frantically greeted them both. This somehow made Marcus and Cassandra laugh all the harder.

"See? What can be so bad about a little dog?" said Cassandra.

Marcus tried to stifle his laughter long enough to say, "Um, pee on carpets? Despite having to be let outside 100 times a day?"

Giulio smiled at this one, forced to admit it was true.

"Scared to go down but stupid enough to go upstairs?" Marcus added. And all the Federicis nodded in reluctant acceptance of this additional truth. Crescendo was neurotically timid around stairs.

"And in the case of little Crescendo here, she's even afraid of her food bowl!" This struck Marcus as particularly funny and he let loose more laughter as he said it. This was also true. Crescendo would haltingly sneak up on her food, reaching her neck to its farthest extent in an apparent attempt to keep her body as far from the dangerous bowl as possible. She would manage to grab one nugget of food and scurry away with it in abject fear.

Cassandra was wiping tears from her eyes as she and her parents again were forced to acknowledge the truth of Marcus's claims. "Yes, but, look how cute she is!" Cassandra countered.

"Ha! So as long as someone is cute, that excuses the fact that they go to the bathroom on your carpets?" Marcus raised his eyebrows to emphasize his triumphant point.

"When that someone is our dear little Crescendo, absolutely! Just look at what a good job she does greeting us! Look! She is so happy to see you!" said Cassandra.

As if right on cue, Crescendo stood with her front paws on Marcus's leg to reach his hand and lick it, tail wagging rhythmically.

"I think it's an international canine conspiracy. The dogs have *us* trained!" cried Marcus. "All they have to do is look cute and greet us as if we've come back from the dead every time we enter the house. And their reward? They get to live indoors, sleep on our furniture and beds, eat free food, and do no work. We'll pay expensive vet bills to have them cared for, and on and on. It's the perfect setup."

"Ah, yes, but maybe there is a lesson in there for us somewhere," countered Giulio. "Maybe if we could be so sincerely excited to see people and give them unconditional love, maybe our lives would be a bit easier, too, no?"

"So little Crescendo here hasn't won you over to the dog side?" asked Stefania.

"Not yet," answered Marcus, "but she's making it tougher and tougher for me to hold out."

Cassandra and Marcus gradually got control of their gleeful silliness, and joined Giulio and Stefania at the table, full of conversation about their day. They related the sights they had seen, and Cassandra's parents asked Marcus about his impressions.

"I think I liked the Villa Aldobrandini the best. The views from up there, as Cassandra had promised, were amazing. And I love how it was so quiet walking around that old villa, nothing but the sound of the gravel crunching under our feet, looking out over the city and Rome in the far distance below. Amazing. It makes me think about whoever picked that spot positioned the building that way, the whole thing. Beautiful. All of it. There is something about the way you Italians make things. You do it right!" Marcus looked at Cassandra as he spoke, and his meaning was not lost on Giulio or Stefania. Abruptly, Giulio excused himself, got up from the table, and left the room.

Stefania immediately took control of the conversation, and Marcus wondered if she was covering Giulio's abrupt departure. "Giulio had a good video chat with that young lady you connected him with about Bitcoin," she said.

"Katya. Good," said Marcus. "I was wondering how that went."

"Yes, I think he enjoyed it. She said to tell you 'hi,' Cassandra."

"I love Katya," answered Cassandra, holding Marcus's hand under the table.

"Giulio sure has taken an interest in this Bitcoin," added Stefania. "He's always a curious student."

Marcus nodded and smiled, and now wondered to himself if Stefania knew about his plans and the agreement with Giulio. He thought about what she had just said and about her behavior the past several days, but couldn't seem to come to a conclusion one way or the other. He realized he had taken it for granted that she *did* know, assuming that with a marriage as solid as theirs, Giulio would have told her immediately. But maybe that wasn't right. Maybe she didn't know. After all, he thought, he really didn't know these people that well yet. There was a slight cultural barrier, and he couldn't be sure how Giulio would have behaved in this situation.

So in the event that Stefania *didn't* know, what did that imply? Did it possibly mean that Giulio wasn't going to come through and give Marcus his blessing? Did it mean Giulio had kept it from Stefania because he had never intended to give Marcus his consent in the first place? Or perhaps Giulio would honor the agreement, but saw no possibility he would fully understand and become passionate about Bitcoin? For the next few minutes while the conversation ran on without him, Marcus mulled over the situation repeatedly, inspecting it from every angle like an ancient glass artifact held up to the light. Every angle resulted in the same conclusion: if Stefania didn't know about his intentions and the agreement with Giulio, that could only be bad. Because truly, wouldn't Marcus need to secure Stefania's blessing, too? Could a marriage to their one and only wonderful daughter really occur without Stefania being all-in on the groom as well? Marcus's previously joyful mood faded as he struggled to figure out what to do next.

23

The next morning Marcus and Cassandra returned from their run and Giulio summoned Marcus onto the back patio. Cassandra excused herself and went upstairs to shower, and Marcus felt his tongue dry against the side of his mouth as he crossed through the double kitchen doors into the mid-morning sunlit deck. He wiped the sweat from his brow and stood looking at Giulio, letting his heart rate come down.

"Price action," said Giulio motioning to the open lounge chair next to his. Marcus thought Giulio's voice had an edge to it but couldn't be sure.

"Yes?"

"I think finally it came down to price action," said Giulio.

Marcus sat sideways and upright on the side of the lounge chair, still sweating. Only now he wasn't sure all the sweating was because of his recent exercise. He proceeded carefully.

"OK, I'm not sure I follow what you mean."

"Katya, your friend, the cute blonde you put me on video call with yesterday. She's a sharp knife," said Giulio, and Marcus realized it was the first time he had noticed Giulio mishandle an English slang term. To the now paranoid Marcus, it was a second data point in as many seconds that Giulio was off his game for some reason.

"I'm glad you liked her, and yes, she knows her stuff. Was she helpful in answering your question?" asked Marcus.

"Yes, she was. She gave me the broad sweep from the early days to the present, explained once again how mining impacts things, and told me some interesting stories about some of the early days. I now think I grasp how Bitcoin went from an experiment to a worldwide thing."

"That's great," said Marcus.

"And ultimately, the more I thought about it, the more I realized that eventually price action drove its wide acceptance. You cannot consistently increase in value, at what, an average of 200 percent or more each year, without attracting a lot of attention. To be honest, I'll bet more and more people were brought in due to the interesting price action than anything else. And then, maybe like me, as they dug in and came to understand Bitcoin a little bit, they got interested in the rest," explained Giulio, who was curiously not looking directly at Marcus but only glancing at him intermittently.

Marcus almost asked, "And are you interested in the rest?" This was the dominant thought on his mind, but somehow, through massive willpower, he refrained from saying anything at all.

Giulio continued, "I want to know more about this part of it; namely, why is Bitcoin going up so much and where do the experts expect it to go? Is it just a mania, a bubble? Or is it even too late to get in on the action?"

"OK, let's talk about that. It's one of my favorite parts of Bitcoin. I can't remember if we covered this yet—about money being three things? Number one: a store of value; number two:

a medium of exchange; and number three: a unit of account."

"Yes, we did. And Katya did, too," answered Giulio.

"Well, I believe Bitcoin was created with the intention of becoming all three, and it might be on its way to accomplishing all three at some point in the future. But for whatever set of reasons, at this point it seems to be largely lodged in number one, a store of value. And as such, because of its preprogrammed and immutable scarcity, and its known and unchangeable monetary policy, it is more than just a store of value but also a way to grow wealth, by the price action you mentioned." Marcus knew he was talking too much, that he should be slowing down and encouraging the engagement of Giulio more, but something in Giulio's behavior was making him nervous and he tried to cover it up, which made it worse.

"Think about this," Marcus continued. "The 'store of value' application might be the biggest total addressable market on the planet! As a category, it is enormous. How many total dollars or euro do you think people have tucked away in mattresses, safes, safe deposit boxes, bank accounts? In addition to this, there are those who hold gold, silver, gems, precious art, real estate, bonds, you name it. These are all purchased with the idea of them holding their value—"

"Or going up," interrupted Giulio.

"Exactly. And don't just think of individuals, think of institutions. So how big is the world's 'store-of-value' market? It's got to be hundreds of *trillions* of dollars! This means that if people continue to wake up to Bitcoin as the best store of value ever on offer to the human race, the demand for it will be astronomical. And with an enormous and increasing demand, placed against a limited and unchangeable supply, what happens to the price?"

"It goes way up."

"Way up," confirmed Marcus. "It's what some call *number-go-up technology*. Better technologies always steal market share from lesser technologies, and if Bitcoin is the best money technology to ever come along, and specifically the best store-of-value technology, how much of the older more clunky and less effective store-of-value technologies like cash and gold and silver and you name it will be displaced into Bitcoin instead?"

"Tons," said Giulio, looking more and more at Marcus now.

"Literally! Take gold, which is measured in tons. The world's total known above-ground gold supply is worth about $11 trillion as we speak. Ari just texted me that yesterday. If that is the case and Bitcoin displaced just gold, and nothing else, as a store of value, then the price of bitcoin would have to grow over *ten times* from where it is today! This is a possibility put forward by the Winklevoss twins, who famously helped invent Facebook but were forced out by Zuckerberg, only to later discover Bitcoin early and become some of the world's wealthiest Bitcoiners. They put forward the idea that if Bitcoin replaced only gold, it would be around an $11 trillion market cap, which is many times larger than it is today."

"It sounds preposterous to talk about multipliers that big, but that's actually sound reasoning," nodded Giulio.

"Totally. So you've got a superior store-of-value technology and, as would be predicted, a rapidly growing market share. It's possibly the largest total addressable market anywhere, meaning that Bitcoin in this use case hasn't really even gotten started yet. And, think of this! Usually, the big money boys of Wall

Street are the early movers on great investment ideas, and the little guy, who is derogatorily called—"

"Dumb money," interrupted Giulio.

"Right, the dumb money, gets to the table last and has to be satisfied with the scraps. What we are seeing with Bitcoin is the exact opposite. It was discovered by the little guy, individuals everywhere, and has moved into the bigger and bigger players in the world of money getting involved, from hedge fund managers to endowments to sovereign wealth funds. Now, there have been corporate treasurers adding Bitcoin to their balance sheets. And some Bitcoiners are predicting that as an uncorrelated asset with undeniable growth possibilities, Bitcoin could even be added to the balance sheets of central banks!"

"Ha! Wouldn't that be ironic," said Giulio, whose usual good mood was seemingly returning.

"Very. It's an uncorrelated asset, meaning, its price doesn't follow the stock market, nor the bond market, nor anything else, so it is very useful to big investors to help them diversify their portfolios.

"The key to remember is that all of this is predicated on a real, fundamental reason. It is not irrational exuberance. Bitcoin has grown so much because of what it offers to the world. At its root it is the best store of value ever. And it gives people freedom over their money and allows them to take a financial step away from the overreach of big government."

"And it's not in a bubble?" asked Giulio.

"No. Now, don't get me wrong. Bitcoin's price has always been very volatile. Bitcoin skies to new heights, then has these huge pullbacks that people call *bitcoin winters*. But then it races way upward to new records. But if you zoom out for the long-term view, it trends steeply upward and to the right.

"This behavior is normal for a new technology, by the way. Bubbles don't pop only to rise again higher in the following years. You know what *does* behave that way? New technologies whose times have come, as we saw with companies like Amazon and Apple, for example. If you look at their stock price histories, you'll see very volatile ups and downs and specific times when, if the game had stopped, you would have said that they had been a bubble."

"But they weren't because they came roaring back again," added Giulio.

"And then beyond, much beyond, their previous highs. Who wouldn't want to go back in time and load up on Amazon stock in say 1998, or Apple just before Steve Jobs returned to the company? I firmly believe—and I'm in good company here—I firmly believe that we are in those kinds of early days with Bitcoin. I could be wrong, of course, but what about this: Let's say someone were to put just 1 percent of their portfolio in Bitcoin. If the value of Bitcoin grew by 100 percent over the next however many years, as some of the models are predicting, that person would have doubled their net worth. If we are all completely wrong and it collapsed somehow and went to zero, that person would hardly notice."

"That's pretty good thinking, Marcus, I like that."

"Thanks, but it's not mine. I stole it from an author named Matthew Kratter. I thought it was so good I repeat it all the time! But actually, world-renowned investor Paul Tudor Jones says he put 5 percent of his portfolio in Bitcoin. The same principles apply, but that would give a much bigger return should the positive upside for Bitcoin prove true.

"Well, so now you are familiar with *Bitcoin maximalization*. It's the view that bitcoin will eventually become the world's reserve currency and all other money systems will be built upon it. This view says that Bitcoin has so many upward potentialities that one should buy and hang on to it for the long term. There is actually a funny term in the Bitcoin world called 'HODL', and it comes from a typo in which someone meant to say HOLD. Someone else chimed in and said it must be an acronym for 'hold on for dear life.'"

"That's a good saying for long-term investing," added Giulio.

"Absolutely. Find an overwhelmingly good value story, do your own research, and if you become convinced, buy in bigtime and hold for the long term."

Cassandra stepped onto the patio, cleaned up from her run and smelling wonderful. Marcus took note of her flattering white cotton skirt and sleeveless blouse. He couldn't help but hear his own words echoing in his ears and thought once again how much he ached to invest for the long term in this terrific person. He had found an overwhelmingly good value story, and was readier than ever to HODL .

24

Marcus was eventually able to dismiss himself to his room and clean up for the day, and while doing so, he carefully extracted the engagement ring from a compartment inside his suitcase. He opened the jeweler's box and admired the sparkly diamond. It cost considerably more than he had originally intended when secretly shopping for a ring, but he had found this particular stone in this setting and knew it was the right one for Cassandra. He was sure she would prefer a complete surprise rather than be involved in ring shopping. He was also confident she shared his feelings and would say yes to becoming his wife. What he was not so certain of, however, was how he and his plans presently stood with the Federici parents.

Cassandra had been thoughtful of Marcus's time while in Italy, was eager to act the tour guide, and did so deftly without overscheduling. Today, however, they had a big day planned. She would take Marcus to Tivoli, a town northeast of Rome overflowing with attractions. It featured the enormous ruins of Hadrian's Villa, which covered hundreds of hectares and consisted of pools, palaces, temples, outdoor dining rooms, and over thirty buildings in all. Cassandra knew that Marcus appreciated architecture, and Hadrian's villa was a wonder in that regard. Hadrian had been one of the most well-traveled of the emperors, and had dictated that many of the architectural styles he had appreciated on his travels be incorporated onto his property. While they all lay in ruins, there remained many partial structures that presented more fascination than could really be appreciated in one visit. The town of Tivoli itself also featured Roman baths, churches, and natural beauties galore. There was no way they could take it all in in one day, especially given their slightly late start. This made them all the more eager to be under way.

As Marcus and Cassandra backed out of the gravel driveway, Marcus pondered again his chances with Giulio and bringing his marriage plans to fruition. He decided to get additional help with the project, and texted Ari a message, telling him to be ready for a call. Satisfied he had done all he could for the moment, Marcus tucked his phone into the side pocket of his shorts and cleared his head in order to get the most enjoyment out of the exciting day ahead. He reached for Cassandra's hand as she shifted through the gears and leaned over to kiss her on the cheek.

***

Back at the Federici home, after a leisurely breakfast and conversation with Stefania, Giulio took his laptop computer to the back patio and made himself comfortable on his usual lounge chair. He opened his internet browser and began to search.

***

Late that evening Cassandra and Marcus arrived back home to a dark and quiet house. Exhausted from an adventurous day and deeply happy from more memories made together, they embraced tenderly, kissed for a moment, and then parted for the night.

Having agreed to skip the next morning's run on account of their late arrival the night before, Cassandra and Marcus both slept in. Marcus was up first and found Giulio in the same spot on the patio where, unbeknownst to Marcus, Giulio had spent most of the previous day. Stefania was nowhere in sight. Crescendo, however, scampered quickly onto the scene and jumped up on the chair with Marcus.

"*Buongiorno*, young Marcus. Did my daughter run your wheels off yesterday? You guys must have gotten in late," Giulio said.

"*Buongiorno*, good morning. Yes, Tivoli was incredible! I think I would need a week there to even scratch the surface. My eyes have seen more beauty this week than they have my whole life, I think."

"Ah, I see you have been bitten by the Italy bug, then! Yes, I am glad you enjoyed yourself. Tivoli is nice. But Tivoli is not the only Italian beauty you are fascinated with," said Giulio in a tone Marcus could not discern.

Marcus felt himself blushing and grinned. "You know how I feel about your daughter, sir," he answered carefully.

"Just so. Just so," said Giulio lifting himself off the lounge chair and retrieving his laptop from the kitchen. "While you lovebirds were out frolicking yesterday, I took it upon myself to continue my Bitcoin education."

Marcus remained silent, sensing from Giulio's curious tone that he, Marcus, had walked into an ambush of some sort.

"Not everyone, it seems, is quite so enamored with Bitcoin as are you," Giulio said.

"No, of course not," answered Marcus, shifting his weight in the chair and struggling to know where to rest his hands. He tried to appear as casual as possible but could feel his heartbeat accelerating. His mind was drawing conclusions from Giulio's behavior that his heart didn't want to face.

"Perhaps you can answer me some questions, then?" said Giulio, his voice still kind but his gaze unyielding.

"Of course," Marcus replied. "Ask me anything."

"Unfortunately, I don't have time right now. I've got to go up to Bergamo today to our church plant there. I'll be gone about three days. Lord willing, we can dig into Bitcoin again when I get back."

"Sure."

Just then Cassandra appeared and sat down next to Marcus on his lounge. "You're off to Bergamo today?" she asked of Giulio, confirming.

"Yes, and actually, I'm running late," said Giulio getting up, kissing her on the top of the head and heading into the house. "You kids take care."

After Giulio left the patio, Cassandra gave Marcus a good morning kiss and looked at him strangely afterwards. "What's wrong?" she asked.

"Oh, nothing," answered Marcus, pondering Giulio's mood. Quickly, he made a calculation of what time it was back in Pittsburgh, concluded that it was too early to call Ari just yet, forced a smile to his face, and said, "What's on the agenda for today?"

"Well, since Papa will be gone, I don't think you'll be forced to talk Bitcoin! I'm so sorry, I had no idea he would make you talk about your work so much."

"I don't mind at all. He's just showing an interest in me," covered Marcus, but he could tell she wasn't convinced and that her quick mind was analyzing the situation.

After a moment she said, "Today can be a lazy day if you wish, or we can do some more touring. This evening I have a gathering of my friends coming over. Everyone wants to meet you!"

Glad of the subject change, Marcus inquired about these friends, asking her to remind him who was who and which person went with what story he had heard. Apparently one or two ex-boyfriends would also be in the mix, and Marcus prepared himself for the unwelcome competition. Eventually, they walked into town to visit Cassandra's favorite bakery and also to the vegetable and fruit stands to pick up some items for Stefania. In this way the next several hours passed peacefully, but Marcus's mind was working in the background all the while.

Finally, early afternoon arrived, and Marcus decided Ari was likely to be awake back in the States. Ari was one of the most enthusiastic Bitcoin maximalists Marcus knew, and Marcus was itching to have him speak directly with Giulio the way Katya had. He had texted Ari with the general idea the previous day. Now he had the specifics. He would have Ari address the common objections about Bitcoin.

Once Marcus and Cassandra returned from town, Marcus slipped away to his room and called Ari to get him apprised of the situation. Marcus was left to guess the timing of the call, so he implored Ari to be ready at any time of day or night to accept it.

"OK, buddy, I'll do this for you. But don't you think it would just be easier to get Cassandra involved?" asked Ari.

"No way, man. I'm not going to blow this surprise. I've worked too hard on this. You're the key now."

"Dang, no pressure!"

"Sorry dude, but I know you're up to it," Marcus assured him. "It's just so weird, though, Ari. I mean, Giulio was downright enthusiastic when we were talking about the total addressable market of Bitcoin as a store of value worldwide. It felt like everything was falling into place. The problem during those days was that Cassandra was getting annoyed with me talking Bitcoin with her father all the time and kind of leaving her out. Now it's the opposite. I've got things patched up with her but now her dad's gotten all gruff about Bitcoin. He's definitely been acting strange. It's almost as if he doesn't *want* to be interested in it."

"Of course he doesn't want to be interested in it. He probably realized he was getting excited about Bitcoin, like all of us do when we dig into it and begin to really understand it. It probably dawned on him that his enthusiasm meant he was going to lose his daughter."

"He isn't going to *lose* her!" said Marcus.

"Sure, you and I don't see it that way, but you gotta realize, she's his only little girl. And they strike me as a tight, classic family. You're probably breaking his heart!"

Marcus considered this and was quiet. He hadn't seen things from Giulio's perspective enough to comprehend what was going on. All he had been focusing on was what he, himself wanted. He had been so blinded by his love for Cassandra that he hadn't adequately empathized with what Giulio was going through. "You're right, Ari. That's it."

"You ask me, bud, your task has never really been to sell Giulio on Bitcoin. Your task has been to sell him on *you!*"

Marcus looked down and rubbed his forehead. "You're the best, Ari. Thanks for the perspective. Really. But this doesn't mean I don't still need you to talk to him and give me the assist of a lifetime."

"I will, man, I will. Just tell me when," said Ari.

25

I'm going to try and phone a friend for this one," Marcus said to Giulio four days later as he pressed Ari's avatar on speed dial. Giulio and Marcus were seated in their now usual spots on the lounges on the back patio, getting caught up on each other's activities of late and transitioning back to Bitcoin. Crescendo was nestled in Marcus's lap, as had become the norm. It was mid-morning, definitely not the ideal time for calling the United States, but Marcus felt he had no choice. It was time to put Giulio in front of the best.

The video chat ring tone continued for what seemed a month as Marcus grinned sheepishly at the now curious face of Giulio. Nothing. The ringing stopped and the attempted call ended. Marcus swallowed hard.

"Um, let me just try him once again," he said.

"Are you calling someone in the United States?" asked Giulio.

Marcus nodded.

"It's late in the night for them, or super early morning," Giulio said.

Marcus nodded again, willing Ari to answer the stupid phone! The familiar sound of a call connecting made him glance down to see that Ari had indeed picked up. Marcus felt a real sense of inward relief.

"Dude, just a minute," said a groggy sounding Ari. The screen was too dark to see anything except occasional glimpses of reflected light off Ari's face. He was obviously moving, likely making his way out of bed and toward a light switch.

Marcus tried to play it cool. "Hey, Ari, it's Marcus. Thanks for picking up," he said in the most casual tone he could muster.

"Yeah, no problem man, just a minute," said the screen, which was followed by rustling sounds and then the bright flash of a light as Ari apparently finally found the switch. "Ok, dude, what can I do for ya?"

"Well, I'm sitting here with Cassandra's dad, Giulio Federici. Giulio, meet Ari," Marcus said, turning the phone screen to face Giulio.

"Hey, Ari, it's a pleasure to meet you! So sorry your friend here woke you up in the night!" said Giulio, gregarious as ever upon meeting someone. Giulio's mood since returning from his trip had been cheerful, and he had only minutes ago brought up the subject of Bitcoin for the first time since his return the day before.

"Nice to meet you, sir," said Ari, gradually coming to life.

"So," said Marcus, "Giulio and I have been discussing Bitcoin a lot since I've been over here, and, um, I think we've covered a lot of ground. We've been through the 'why' of Bitcoin, meaning, the problem that it was invented to solve, and the 'what it is' and a bunch of the 'how it works.' We also have discussed how huge Bitcoin could and should become. Now Giulio has some questions about some of the, what might I call them? 'Yeah, buts.'"

"OK, OK, sure. Yeah, there are some really good pushbacks on Bitcoin that sound pretty plausible until you dig into them. Mr. Federici, I'll do my best to answer any questions you have. Go ahead," said Ari politely.

"OK," said Giulio. "The biggest concern I keep reading about is how much electricity is consumed in the mining of Bitcoin. All of this huge computing power of these miners competing to write the next blocks onto the blockchain is sucking up a lot of electricity. The amount is even comparable to the usage of some small countries."

"To begin," said Ari, "I am going to quote a really good book about Bitcoin called *Thank God for Bitcoin*. In it the authors say, 'Bitcoin is a non-inflatable money in a world where wealth is continuously stolen by inflation.' Think about that for a moment. And consider this: every fiat currency in world history has been debased to a fraction of its original value. Every single one. No exceptions. In considering the broken money that is used all over the entire earth, what would it be worth to have something that is non-inflatable? What would we pay to stop a worldwide heist? Would it be worth the consumption of some of the earth's bountiful energy? That is the first thing to consider: that having a money like this that fixes the global theft happening invisibly every day through inflation is worth its cost. We should expect to pay something in order to have and maintain the greatest 'fairness' revolution in the history of money.

"Now, given that, let's consider its 'cost,' which really means its consumption of energy. We are not running out of energy. There is no energy shortage. Energy is indescribably abundant on the earth. Our planet is radiated with thousands of times more than we need every day. Most of it goes unused because we don't capture or utilize even the tiniest fraction of it. Sunshine, wind, water movement, all these provide clean, renewable sources of energy that largely go untapped. Then there are the fossil fuels that many people don't like but others refer to as nature's battery. Yes, energy is abundant and available in so many forms.

"Some say that Bitcoin is actually good for the environment because it is driving the adoption of renewables faster than they otherwise would be adopted with a real-world use for their output that can be located near them. This is a much more effective way to promote their spread than government subsidies and mandates. The estimates are that over 73 percent of the electricity used for Bitcoin is already renewable energy, and that percentage is growing. Jack Dorsey, the founder of Twitter and CEO of Square, predicted that Bitcoin would eventually run on 100 percent renewable energy.

"But not just *renewable* energy, *wasted* energy, too. For instance, the country of El Salvador plans to use the electricity generated by volcanoes to mine Bitcoin, which is an extreme example. More commonly, have you ever driven by an oil field and seen a continual flame coming out of a pipe?"

"Yes," answered Giulio.

"That's called flaring. When oil companies drill for crude oil, they also get natural gas as a byproduct. If there is no pipeline nearby to carry it to market, they just burn it off. It is wasteful, and also creates carbon dioxide emissions. If they don't flare it then it gets released directly into the atmosphere as methane, which is also bad for the environment."

"OK."

"Well, Bitcoin miners have put together portable rigs that can be pulled by trucks up to these locations and convert this gas to electricity to power their computers, right on the spot. This is just one way in which Bitcoin miners are capturing energy that is otherwise wasted and harmful."

"That's clever."

"Now let's consider the energy consumption of Bitcoin and compare it to the system it is competing against. How much energy is used in running the world's fiat currency systems? Think of the energy cost of everything required to run a huge government bureaucracy, central banking system, and governments strong enough to force people to use a money that steals from them every day. What about 80,000 bank branches in the US alone? Or some of the tallest skyscrapers or most opulent headquarters buildings? Or what about this: the fiat money system, since the creation of the Federal Reserve in 1913, has caused a recession on average every 5 or 6 years, as the Fed's money creation drives the boom-bust cycle. Each recession destroys trillions in wealth that required huge amounts of resources to create. That's wasted carbon every time. Is that 10,000 times more harmful to the environment than Bitcoin? 100,000 times? 1,000,000 times? Higher?

"Or let's simply compare bitcoin to gold. You don't hear many people railing against gold's energy consumption. The estimated annual energy required for gold mining, storage, and transport is over twice the amount for Bitcoin.

"The final thing I'd say on this is that we should approach this fairly. If we're concerned about electricity consumption, how do the rest of the things we do stack up? One estimate said that Bitcoin consumes less energy than the clothes dryers in the United States. What about the vampire power or standby power or leaking energy, whatever term you want to use, for all of our electronics? This is the electricity gadgets waste just by being plugged in when they are not in use. In the United States, 25 percent of electricity used by home electronics occurs while products are switched off. Is anybody attacking electronic devices because they waste energy even when not in use? Or consider video gaming, which is an enormous consumer of energy. A study found that the PC gamers in the US use the equivalent of the output of 25 electric power plants. Twenty-five! And to what purpose? Having fun?

"Also, you don't hear any of these investors who are so concerned about ESG investing—"

"What's that?" interrupted Giulio.

"It stands for Environment, Social, and Governance. This means companies that demonstrate care for the environment, embrace social issues, and have diversity in their board of directors and executive ranks. The concept of investing in ESG compliant companies has caught on in Wall Street. But the point I was going to make is that all of these funds that claim an interest in ESG still buy Google stock. And Google owns YouTube, and YouTube uses a whopping 2.5 percent of the world's energy."

"They do?" asked Giulio.

"Yes. It's an enormous amount. But nobody has politicized that and held it against them."

"That's a key point, Ari," said Giulio. "There doesn't seem to be any consistency of what gets criticized and what gets accepted or ignored. Like everything else, it seems to follow emotions instead of logic."

"Yes, Mr. Federici, that's totally correct. People buy into one central narrative, an oversimplified one at that, and don't stop to consider its inconsistencies or conflicts."

"OK, so Bitcoin's energy use?" asked Giulio, with a tone of voice that suggested he wanted a summary.

"So when you consider the humongous good that Bitcoin brings to the world, and compare it against the abundance of energy that we have available to us if we made the effort to harness it, or if you compare its energy usage to the much more wasteful fiat currency system it is competing against, or if you think about all the much larger wastes of energy we have around us all the time, it becomes clear that Bitcoin is accomplishing a lot for very little. The facts present a case almost exactly opposite of the criticisms uninformed people wage against it. The concern about Bitcoin's energy consumption is a 'truthy' thing, which means it sounds plausible at first, but when you dig into it and analyze it logically, it doesn't hold up."

"OK, yeah, those are good points, Ari. Thank you. But didn't Elon Musk say Bitcoin was bad for the environment?"

"Musk is an interesting case. He came out as a huge supporter of Bitcoin, and his company, Tesla, bought a large amount for its corporate treasury, which Musk said they would not sell. And they even began accepting Bitcoin toward the purchase of Tesla cars. But then months later he abruptly flipped and said they would no longer sell cars for Bitcoin because he was concerned for the environment.

"I think it might be because he received pressure from extremists who won't listen to the facts about Bitcoin's energy consumption, and he got worried it would hurt car sales, or his brand, or whatever. That's my take on it at least. Only Musk

knows for sure. But I think it's one of the only ways to understand it. He realized that his newfound fascination with Bitcoin put him in a position of having to explain that Bitcoin is
not bad for the environment, and that's a nuance that doesn't
sell as easily as 'electric cars will save the planet and if not, I'll
build rockets to take everyone to Mars.'"

"Yeah, that is how he presents himself," said Giulio.

"But it could be that Musk is being clever, and he'll later
announce that he's gone into Bitcoin mining in a totally green
way. That is the real future of Bitcoin, and Musk could help
lead that effort. I guess that would be another interpretation of
his comments. And it would be kind of typical of his unpre-
dictability and tendency to pump for things he's investing in,
really. And anyway, he came off of some of his statements later,
and even opened the buying of Teslas back up to Bitcoin again,
so there's no telling what's really going on in his mind. I should
also say that he deserves credit for being one of the world's first
corporate billionaires to buy into Bitcoin in a big way.

"Finally, let's not forget about the big picture here. The energy usage of Bitcoin only adds up to about 0.1% of the world's
total energy consumption. That is a negligible amount."

"Ok," said Giulio. "I think I understand all you've explained here. And it's pretty clear Bitcoin is way bigger than
any one man. One thing I read that presents the amount of
energy in Bitcoin from a different perspective is this: isn't it
true, that the higher the overall hash power, the more secure
the Bitcoin network?"

"Yes, exactly. Some say that Bitcoin is protected by a *wall
of energy*. And most of that energy is used at the margins of
the grid, meaning the places where it would be wasted any-

way if not used by Bitcoin miners. But it's the sheer volume of this energy that makes Bitcoin impregnable, and that is what we should want for the thing that protects the value of all the world's money. Think about it. If energy is one of, if not the most abundant thing around us, and Bitcoin is protected by energy, then it has an almost infinite expandability in its security as it grows over time. If it were protected by something more limited, it couldn't survive long term, because that limit would eventually be reached. But because it's protected by something as endless as the light from the sun or wind and waves, Bitcoin has unlimited upward security."

"Speaking of that," said Giulio, "what about quantum computers? I read that their computational power could overwhelm Bitcoin's cryptography."

"Well, quantum computers are still very much in the laboratory as an exploratory concept. But, if they do prove out to actually work someday, and that is not a given, there is already quantum cryptography being developed. It's always the way things go. Better thieves lead to better locks. Why would that not be the case here? Also, wouldn't Bitcoin be *defended* by quantum computers, too? That's a more accurate representation of how technology comes to pass; hackers on both sides escalate the war in real time as advancements come and weaponry advances. New missiles lead to improved missile defense systems. And, if quantum computing should really come to pass, there are much easier and more lucrative targets than Bitcoin for them to go after. The central banks of all the nations, for instance. That is where they would likely start. But this is all hypothetical."

Cassandra entered and recognized the voice on the phone.

She bent down behind Giulio so her face would be included on the screen and greeted Ari.

"What time is it over there?" she asked Ari.

"Oh, I think it's o-dark-thirty, or thereabouts," he replied.

"Sorry, buddy. These two men of mine seem to have Bitcoin on the brain!" Cassandra said.

"It's perfectly alright. I figure if someone as influential as your dad becomes a Bitcoiner, there would be little we could do more important for the cause of financial justice!" said Ari.

"Ah, flattery will get you nowhere, my boy," said Giulio.

"Ok, well, good to see you Ari. Take care," she said. "Ciao!"

"Ciao, Cassandra. Bye," Ari replied.

Cassandra then took Marcus's hand and led him indoors to the kitchen. She reminded him that it was time for them to go over to Nonna's house and take her on a walk, and then join her afterward for lunch. "She is making her famous gnocchi just for you," she said. "It's a recipe that has been in our family for generations." Marcus nodded and went back to the patio to excuse himself.

"You'll be in good hands, Giulio. Ari is more informed about Bitcoin than anybody I know," Marcus said.

"You're leaving us? But I've got your phone," protested Giulio. In the meantime, Marcus could see the all-knowing look on Ari's face on the screen.

"Oh, that's right. I'll text Ari your number and he can call you directly," Marcus said taking the phone from Giulio. "Have fun with Ari. And hey, Ari—thanks a lot for your time. Sorry again it's so early for you."

Ari gave a conspiratorial grin, and nodded as if to say, 'you owe me one.' Then he said, "No problem. Giulio and I here will have some fun. Go and enjoy yourself."

26

So where are you from?" Giulio asked Ari once they'd reconnected.

"I was born in Syria but lived for almost ten years in Venezuela. My dad is a petroleum engineer and we moved there with his job."

"But you're in the States, now, right?"

"Yes. I'm based in Pittsburgh. I'm actually Marcus's roommate."

"And your parents, are they still in Venezuela?" Giulio asked.

"No, thankfully. They're now here in the United States, down in Texas. The situation in Venezuela got so bad they had to get out. We were the lucky ones, I guess, being foreigners, it was easier for us to leave when the currency collapsed. But the citizens of Venezuela, they've had it hard. Many have lost everything. In 2014 the supply of the bolivar increased by 64 percent, then 111 percent more in 2016. That's when we left. But it has continued. It grew another 96 percent the next year. The currency inflates so quickly that people have to spend it to buy something of value as soon as they get it. Our neighbor had a small motorcycle shop, and he was forced to put all his life savings into crates and crates of motorcycles because they were the quickest thing he had access to that held actual, real value. It's nuts."

"Oh, man. I have heard that the situation is not a good one," said Giulio.

"Yes, people don't really understand, I don't think, how hard life is when the government ruins the money. It's not a theoretical thing, it's real life. And actual suffering. It's why I studied economics when I got here. I wanted to learn what had happened to the country I grew up in," explained Ari. "Now I know. It's one of the reasons I'm so passionate about Bitcoin. As they say, 'fix the money, fix the world.'"

Giulio considered this and nodded. "We don't have to go through the rest of these questions of mine if you don't want to," he said. "I feel bad keeping you up."

"No, seriously, it's no problem. I'm up now, anyway. And it's funny, I've always said you could wake me up in the middle of the night and I could talk about Bitcoin, and now I'm actually doing it!" said Ari.

"OK, if you're sure."

"Yup, no trouble," he said, sipping coffee.

"Ok, well, the next topic I wrote down is intrinsic value. How are we supposed to think of Bitcoin as having value when it is just software?"

"Really good question. Lots of people get tripped up on this one. But if you think about it, does the money we use today have intrinsic value? The answer is absolutely not. It has no value in and of itself. It only has value because the government forces us to use it as money."

"Right. You wouldn't know this, but Marcus and I have

talked all about this particular subject, and I couldn't agree with you Bitcoiners more about how governments are ripping us off through inflation and the endless cycle of debt the banks create," said Giulio.

"Good. Good. Then you understand. The real truth about money, and this is not obvious until you think about it, is that the best money is the thing that is useless as anything other than money. The more it's used for other things, the less it's useful as money. It's something that the real economists teach. And excuse me, but when I say *real*, I am being a bit snarky, because it is different from the cartoon fakery that masquerades as economics that gets taught in many universities today. Real economics, classical economics, if you will, is best represented by a group of economists that have come to be known as the Austrian School of Economics," explained Ari.

"Yes, I've heard of them."

"Good. So here's one of their main teachings: when it comes to money, people left to their individual actions in a free market will choose their own money, the thing that works best. And from this, *value emerges*. It's not inherent or intrinsic in anything that has ever been used as money. It is emergent among the people due to its properties, as I mentioned. One of those properties is almost always that it doesn't get used for much of anything else. Another property is scarcity, and particularly, continued scarcity through something we call a high stock-to-flow ratio. Stock-to-flow is a measure of how much of a good is available versus how much of it can be obtained. For something to be used as money, it should have a high stock-to-flow ratio."

"Yes, Marcus taught me about that."

"Excellent. So when someone says something can't be money because it has no intrinsic value, they are demonstrating that they really don't understand money at all. So back to Bitcoin. Bitcoin has value because in the marketplace people have agreed that it has value. Period. And they have agreed upon that value because of its characteristics, which are much like gold, except exceedingly better. I believe Marcus already discussed that with you, yes?"

"Yes."

"OK, great. And, there is a funny incident I should tell you about. Do you know the name Alan Greenspan?"

"Yes, he was head of the Federal Reserve in the United States a while back, right?"

"Correct. For twenty years he was in charge of the proverbial printing press, expanding the US money supply precipitously. At one point, he was quoted as saying that the government would never go broke because it could just print more money out of thin air. I am paraphrasing, of course, but that's almost exactly what he said. And then later, in one of the most ironic statements ever, he had the audacity to criticize Bitcoin because it had no intrinsic value."

"That's hilarious!" said Giulio. "Hypocritical, no?"

"I'd say, yes! And he's a guy at the center of money creation who clearly demonstrated that he doesn't actually understand money! Or if he does, then he was being intentionally disingenuous. Either way, not good.

"So I think you see that Bitcoin has value as a money just like any other money that has ever come along and found its way into general usage. So there are two types of money, really. One is chosen by the free market, has little to no intrinsic value, but has properties such as scarcity and continued scarcity. The other one, fiat currency, which is forced upon people by governments, also has no intrinsic value, but is the opposite of scarce and will continue that way. Make sense?"

"Yes, I get this one. And I probably already agreed with it, but you've taught me a lot here just now," said the ever-humble Giulio to a man half his age. "How about governments banning Bitcoin? What about that?"

"I would say that in the early days of Bitcoin, it might have been possible. Especially in the days when the dark web grabbed hold of it as a way to buy and sell illegal things. But gradually more and more mainline people and organizations began using it and forming around it, and it has gone so far out into global society that it would be hard to put that toothpaste back in the tube. In the US there have been rulings classifying Bitcoin as a commodity, and these rulings set legal precedent. In the year 2020 regulators in the US allowed banks to custody Bitcoin. Why would they do that if they were going to make it illegal?

"Things could possibly change, I suppose, but then the question would become one of enforcement. How, exactly, could you shut Bitcoin down? It's in the cloud, it cannot be confiscated, and it's digital. It would require unplugging the internet! While this kind of thing has been attempted in totalitarian countries, the people still find a way to use technology to access Google and Twitter, even though they are outlawed in their countries. Like it or not, governments are unable to completely keep the internet out of the hands of their citizens, and Bitcoin, built on the internet, is the same. Also, I think the main places it is likely to be tried to be banned is in places where the governments have made a total wreck of their currency. Or in totalitarian regimes. Of course they would want to fence off any competitors to the money they are ruining for their own benefit. This only harms their economy, as the rest of the world who can innovate with Bitcoin will do so and take up the slack, leaving the closed-off country behind. So it is so far into the game now that legitimate governments are very unlikely to outright ban it, and illegitimate governments are powerless to truly do so, and the extent to which they do so will only hurt themselves."

"Yes," nodded Giulio, "but more and more rules could be made, and regulations could tighten down on it, right?"

"Of course. Nothing is certain. And governments can do surprising things, especially when their own money monopoly is threatened, but they cannot do *everything*. If you understand the technology of Bitcoin and its decentralized nature, you'll see that it is very unworkable for governments to keep people from it entirely, again, especially at this stage in its development. I predict the opposite will happen. I think central banks will create their own digital currencies, on one hand, which would represent a huge blow to freedom and privacy, by the way. And at the same time, some central banks will see Bitcoin's characteristic as the hardest of assets and begin buying it to add to their own reserves, along with the gold they hold. That would be radical, but I think it is very possible. Even probable. Incidentally, I predict Japan will be the first of the larger developed nations to do so. They are already friendly toward Bitcoin, and doing so might just help them out of the economic malaise they've been in since the early nineties."

"Wait, what did you say about central banks creating their

own digital currencies?" asked Giulio.

"Yeah. This one's scary. What happened is private individuals invented decentralized money, which is Bitcoin. Then a company, Facebook, said *it* wanted to create money, and that was a bridge too far. Governments the world over immediately jumped at that and basically said, 'no way.' One Chinese government official said that the Facebook announcement prodded them into action to get serious about creating their own digital currency. The acronym people are using to describe these is CBDC, which stands for Central Bank Digital Currency. A CBDC is a completely digital, centrally controlled and issued electronic money. It would essentially be the exact opposite of decentralized Bitcoin. No more cash, only digital money on your computer or smart phone. It sounds convenient, actually, and that's probably how they will sell it to us.

"The reason I said these would represent a huge blow to freedom is twofold. One: they would bring total surveillance. Much of our money is already digital. When you spend using your credit cards, for instance, or authorize automatic deductions from your account to pay your bills, these show up as digits in a computer. But we do still have cash, and with cash, nobody knows what you do with it. You have some measure of privacy. But if everything went to a CBDC, basically all money would be digital, and the government would be able to track everything everybody spent everywhere all the time. Loss of freedom number one.

"The second blow to freedom is even worse. Much worse. Surveillance and loss of privacy is bad enough, but this next one comes from the fact that a CBDC would be *programmable*. The government could just confiscate some of your money for whatever reason. Or they could control spending. Maybe when the next COVID-19-type scare comes along, instead of mandating lockdowns on certain businesses, they just program the money to no longer work at, say, bars and restaurants. Or maybe they decide people should only buy 2,000 calories a day for the sake of their health? So your money shuts off if you try to buy more than that at a grocery store. Or what if they decided to control lending, favoring some groups over others? Or what if they had a 'social score' where they deduct money from you because they noticed you didn't give any of your money to government-approved charities and causes? If they noticed you didn't jump on the latest bandwagon of politically correct thought to donate your money accordingly? Or if they noticed that you were giving money to a church? Or that you were using your money for any number of things for which they didn't approve? Or what if they decided to do wealth redistribution, just taking some from everyone and giving it to others directly?"

"Those are scary hypotheticals," said Giulio.

"Yes, and they're only that. Hypothetical. I admit that I'm fear-mongering a bit, here, just to make the point. I'm just making up things that would be *possible* with centralized digital government money. But the problem is once you release a technology that *can* do certain things, it only seems to be a matter of time before those things are actually done. It doesn't happen all at once, of course, or the people would revolt. It comes in stages, almost imperceptibly. It's like that frog sitting in water that heats gradually. He doesn't notice it until it's too late and it's boiling. With government power, once you crack open the door an inch—"

"Governments will always open it as far as they can," said Giulio.

"And convince us that it's temporary, for an emergency, or for our own good."

"Or all three!" said Giulio.

The men were silent for a moment as Giulio thought about all he had just heard, grabbing a pencil and jotting down a few notes to himself. Stefania emerged from the kitchen and settled in on the open lounge chair. Giulio pointed the screen in her direction and made the introductions.

"She has been studying Bitcoin along with me," Giulio announced. Surprised, Ari made a mental note to give Marcus this intel.

27

Stefania slid her chair nearer to Giulio's so she could more easily share the screen with him. Upon so arranging herself, she asked a question of her own.

"So why Bitcoin? What about all these other cryptocurrencies that are out there?" she asked.

Ari nodded and said, "That's a very important question, with a lot of different answers, depending upon whom you ask. My response to it is this: Bitcoin is a very specific technology that was developed to do a certain thing very well. That certain thing is to function as a free and unencumbered money, as a permissionless and unchanging store of value. In short, to be the best 'money' that the world has ever seen. The cumbersome but very clever blockchain technology was crafted precisely to create a decentralized store of value that nobody would be able to tamper with, change the supply of, or otherwise debase. Bitcoin was engineered to be this new type of money that leaves governments and central bankers out of the equation entirely. It started as an experiment and had many flaws in its early days, but ardent followers and talented developers fixed those to the point where it has now done a few very important things. Number one: it has satisfied the law of networks, or Metcalf's

Law, and has by far the largest user base, estimated to be somewhere around 50 million people and growing. Number two: it
has stood the test of time and survived hacks from the outside
and even civil wars from the inside, called forks, which maybe
I can explain later. So it has gained wide usage and has survived
every assault now for over twelve years. It has proven itself to
be, as I said before, the best money for the world."

"But the other cryptocurrencies?" reminded Stefania.

"All the other ones fall short of Bitcoin's specific purpose.
None of them come anywhere near Bitcoin in terms of being
a decentralized money. There are really two types of what we
call 'alternative coins' or 'alt coins.' The first claims to be exactly
what Bitcoin is, only better. The second uses crypto technology
but aims at a different application or purpose. So they all copy
Bitcoin's foundational technology to one degree or another,
and then either straight up try to outdo Bitcoin at being decentralized money, or apply the technology to solving a different
problem. For the ones who claim to be just like Bitcoin except
better, whether it's transaction speed or environmentalism or
whatever, they fall far short of being what Bitcoin is in terms
of an immutable store of value. One of the main reasons is that
they all share a centralized founder, founding group, or enter-
prise. Centralization leads to manipulation. And even some of
the biggest ones of these have gone in and changed the deal
or reversed transactions, thereby showing that they are most
definitely not Bitcoin. These central authorities are also easily
targeted by governments or criminals or terrorists.

"For the alt coins that aim at a different purpose altogether,
there are some interesting problems they are trying to solve.
There are some things that will be fascinating to keep an eye

on. But I should make it clear that almost all of the alt coins are complete trash. They were launched in greed by people who knew they could use tech buzz to sell coins and enrich themselves without bringing anything meaningful to the world."

Stefania then said, "So you don't think Bitcoin could be like MySpace and eventually lose out to a Facebook?"

"No. I've heard that before, and it's a flawed analogy. Bitcoin is to money what the internet was to communication and commerce: a revolutionary base protocol. Just as there is no 'other internet,' there is no 'other Bitcoin.'"

"Wow," said Stefania.

"Yes. The internet—as a base protocol—allowed the building of all of the useful and amazing things we experience today. Bitcoin will be the same. It's the revolutionary foundation that allows all subsequent breakthroughs to be built on top of it."

"Not everyone agrees with that, of course," said Giulio. "In my reading I came across lots of people who think all these other cryptocurrencies are the future."

"True," said Ari. "So let's run with the analogy Stefania mentioned, then. In some ways, all new technology comes on the scene and makes for a Wild West scenario. In the early days of the automobile you had hundreds of car companies, and eventually only a handful won out and lasted for the long term. And yes, there were many attempts at social networking before Facebook took over the world. But for as many stories as there are like that, there are counter-stories. Walmart was the first true 'big box' discount store of its kind, and no one has ever supplanted it. Amazon was the first to do the same online, and again, outside of China, there hasn't been anyone even close. There is nothing that says that the first can't last. And conversely, there is nothing that says that the first is guaranteed to last, either. In the cases where the first has lasted, meaning it has stayed on top, it was because of very specific reasons. And Bitcoin has those reasons.

"It's the most decentralized. It has no central figure or group or authority that can be attacked, arrested, or persuaded. It's the most proven. It's lasted the longest. It's got the biggest amount of involved developers. It's got the largest number of active nodes and the largest total hash power protecting it. It's got the most traction with investors of all stripes. It's the costliest to produce, and therefore the hardest to counterfeit. It has the largest market capitalization. Its monetary policy is the most immutable, and that is probably the most important. It cannot be debased. Its supply is not subject to human tampering or manipulation. While nothing is guaranteed, it seems very unlikely that anything could outpace it in these very important categories. Especially when we are talking about what would make for the world's best money."

"So you don't see any of these other coins becoming big?" asked Stefania.

"Don't get me wrong. I think there will always be other cryptocurrencies around. There will always be someone trying to compete with Bitcoin. And there will also be projects seeking to use this technology for other applications. But long term, I believe you'll see Bitcoin win the race to become the world's first decentralized, nongovernmental, fair money. Actually, I believe Bitcoin already has. Its battle is not really with competitors, now. It's won that battle. Its battle will be with the central banks of the world once they realize how big a threat Bitcoin is to their monopolistic practices."

"And what do you think happens then?" chimed Giulio.

"Again, there are many opinions on this, and nobody can predict the future. It's likely central banks will issue their own digital currencies, as we discussed. But that won't kill off Bitcoin, of course, it will only drive more people to it!

"Ultimately, ideas whose time have come seem to outlive any and all opposition in the end. That's just how things go. Bitcoin is such a good idea for human freedom that I believe it will win out. Governments will have to come to terms with it in one way or another. Some will try to regulate it, which will just force it to grow in other countries where it is welcomed instead. Note El Salvador where it was declared legal tender. Other countries will realize its value and invest in it themselves. And adversarial governments forced to trade with each other may begin to rely on it as a base money between them because they have no trust. And remember? Bitcoin is a trustless system."

"If all that came true, this could be one of the biggest technological advancements of our lifetimes," said Giulio.

"Yes. That is what many of us believe. As I said, what the internet was for information and commerce, Bitcoin will be for money.

"When Goldman Sachs came out and publicly declared Bitcoin a new asset class, one of the comments made was that it's not that often that we get to witness the creation of an entirely new asset class. What a time to be alive!"

"My head hurts," said Stefania playfully.

"Sorry about that!" said Ari.

"The fundamentals of Bitcoin are amazing," said Giulio. "It's easy to just think that there is a world of exciting new technology in the money space, but really, Bitcoin is radically unique."

"Yes!" answered Ari. "Let's go back to the big picture for a moment. Let's think about world views of money. On one hand, we've all grown up in a fiat world view. We have been conditioned all our lives to see everything through the lens of money created and managed and manipulated by the government for its own ends and at our expense. This has given us a world in which we just totally get used to prices going up over time. We are acclimated to money devaluation; to inflation. We think it's normal. Expected. And correct. What this does is make it so nobody *saves*. Instead, you have to *invest* if you are going to have any chance of your money lasting over time. But investing is akin to having another job. It is difficult, takes time, requires a lot of learning, not to mention that investing comes with risk.

"But Satoshi's invention of Bitcoin allows us a brand-new money view. What if people could just save their money and know it would still be good years down the road? And think about this: What if prices for goods and services in the world actually went down over time? Why wouldn't that be a good thing for the individual? We've been conditioned and taught that deflation is some horrible thing, as in, 'Oh no! Our money is actually worth more in the future! How horrible!' Hopefully you can hear my sarcasm!"

"Yes," both Giulio and Stefania said together.

"We have known nothing but money being debased all of our lives and we've come to accept it as normal. But it isn't. It's an enemy. And Satoshi's invention of Bitcoin, which is the separation of money and state, shows us a glimpse of a world in which money can be sound, lasting, and a force for good instead of plunder."

28

So let's review and compare these two money views I've been talking about," said Ari.

"OK," said Giulio, with Stefania nodding along.

"In the fiat world view, we have an inflation of the money supply and resulting prices. In the Bitcoin view, we have a fixed money supply."

"That one we clearly understand," said Giulio.

"In the fiat world it's debt, in the Bitcoin world it's savings."

"Yep."

"Wait, actually, you know what I can do? I've got a chart of this. Let me pull it up on my phone. Hold on a sec. There. Can you guys see that?" Ari said, his screen now fully taken up with a chart.

Fiat Money View	Bitcoin Money View
Inflation	Fixed
Debt	Savings
Unsound	Sound
Centralized	Decentralized
Control	Independence
Contillion Effect	Equality
Elites in Charge	Egalitarianism
Politics	People
Permission Required	Permissionless
Trust Required	Trustless
3rd Party Required	Peer-to-Peer
Censorable	Censorship Resistant

"Yep, we can see it," said Stefania.

"Ok, good, and I'll also send it to you when we're done here."

"Sounds good," said Giulio.

"This chart is something I just hand-drew a while ago. I was trying to capture the difference between what we are used to with the fiat money system and what Bitcoin brings us. As you can see, Bitcoin represents an entirely different philosophy of how money should work. The overarching idea, I would say, is justice. Financial justice."

"I guess people just don't realize how unfair the current fiat system is," said Giulio.

"I think that's because it's invisible, and it is hidden behind purposeful complication."

"Obfuscation," said Giulio.

"Your English is really good, Giulio," said Ari.

"Thank you. I went to university in the States, and I also do all of my fundraising there. So—"

Stefania butted in, "Looking at your list here, and trying to absorb everything Marcus has been teaching us this past week and a half, I feel like this is a reboot of a software program inside of us or something. Would that be a good analogy?"

"That's a great analogy, actually. It's just like downloading an entirely new financial operating system that makes the previous one obsolete. We probably don't even realize how much we've been programmed with the fiat money view throughout our lives. In the Bitcoin world they have a term for it. It goes back to the 1999 movie called *The Matrix*; do you guys know that movie?"

"Of course!" said Giulio. "Take the red pill or the blue pill."

"I can never remember which pill was for what?" said Stefania.

"It was the red pill for truth, honey, and the blue pill for going back into the matrix and ignorant bliss," explained Giulio.

"That's right," said Ari. "Well, in the Bitcoin world, since orange is for some reason its brand color, people liken the awakening to the Bitcoin money view as 'taking the orange pill.'"

"That's good, I like that," said Giulio.

"We'll take some time with this list later," Stefania said, "but since we woke you from your sleep, we'd like to be respectful of your time. Can I ask you one final question?"

"Of course," said Ari.

"What about the accusation I've heard on the news that Bitcoin is just one giant Ponzi scheme?" asked Stefania.

"Well, a true Ponzi scheme is where incredible returns are paid in short timeframes, wherein those returns actually come from new investments coming in, and new money has to be recruited in order to pay out the next returns. Everything appears fine until the new money stops coming in because then no more amazing returns can be paid out. When people are calling Bitcoin a Ponzi scheme, they are actually using the wrong term, since there are no 'returns' on Bitcoin. There is only price movement.

"The more accurate term would be a pyramid scheme. In investing the term is a *pump-and-dump scheme*. Pyramids, or pump-and-dumps, are where you invest early, then do everything possible to promote the asset and get its price to rise, and then sell out later to someone at a much higher price."

"Called the 'greater fool' strategy of investing," said Giulio.

"Correct," said Ari. "Because you may be a fool for buying

in, but as long as greater fools come along later willing to buy the now-inflated asset from you at a higher price, you pocket the difference."

"Yes, I can see why some critics might think Bitcoin is one of those," said Giulio.

"The only thing is, many of the best-informed and biggest holders of bitcoins say they will *never* sell! They comprehend the long-term fundamentals of Bitcoin and realize that to sell would be foolish. If they ever want to 'spend' the value of their bitcoin, they can always borrow against it. But most will never sell. That doesn't sound like a pump-and-dump scheme to me. What would we call it, pump-and-HODL? It's true that's what they are doing, but they will never dump it. So the accusations of pyramid scheme are misplaced. It's definitely a hype-cycle thing, but it's based on underlying fundamentals that won't go away and don't care who understands it or who doesn't. In one communication, Satoshi himself said, 'If you don't believe it or don't get it, I don't have the time to try to convince you, sorry.' And that's what's going on here. The economics and the fundamentals will win out and are blind to incorrect opinions and stubborn so-called experts. Besides, during Bitcoin's life, many have publicly decried it, only to admit later that they were wrong and become enthusiastic about it. Bitcoin has been declared dead more times than I can count, and it always comes roaring back to life, stronger than before."

"OK, well, thank you so much for giving us your time, Ari, especially at such a crazy hour for you. We are very grateful," said Giulio.

"Yes," affirmed Stefania.

"I would do anything for Marcus," said Ari, smiling. "He

is one of the finest people I know. Your daughter is also quite extraordinary, I might add, and I think they make a terrific couple."

"Thank you for your kindness, Ari. It has been a pleasure meeting you. I hope we get to see you in person someday. And if you're ever in Rome…"

29

cassandras parents are great people and smart i think they have
a remarkable understanding of bitcoin for newbies youve done well
also stefania is learning right alongside giulio not sure if you knew
that or not probably means she knows about your arrangement
best of luck with that and you owe me one pal

Marcus read the text coming in from Ari as he and
Cassandra finished their leisurely lunch with Nonna. It was a
typical communication from Ari: brief and to the point, and
entirely absent punctuation or even capital letters. Marcus filed
away the information about Stefania, then returned his phone
to his pocket, making every effort to slow back down to the
pace of life of an octogenarian.

Nonna had a lot to say, as Marcus learned was normal,
and Cassandra translated everything dutifully. There were stories about 'the old country,' which meant Sicily, and tales of
raising Giulio and his younger brother. Giulio's dad featured
in many tales and it became evident that although deceased
for many years, his life still reflected forward with an influence

on his surviving family. The more Marcus heard, the more he thought Giulio must resemble his father in many ways. Nonna confirmed this but indicated that perhaps Giulio was even a little more headstrong.

Eventually Nonna wanted to go for a walk, and Cassandra took her by one arm and Marcus the other. They strolled slowly but impressively far, up and down ancient streets, with Nonna waving and stopping to chat with nearly everyone they encountered. Her hips and knees were bad, but her mind was sharp. For each building or business there was a story, and as they settled on a park bench in one of the piazzas, Nonna pointed to a wine shop that had formerly been a pasticceria. She told of her first boyfriend who had worked there. She couldn't seem to get Marcus's name right, so she just called him 'Marco,' which he didn't mind. As they rested in the afternoon shade, looking out across the larger of the piazzas in Grottaferratta, it dawned on Marcus that this was part of what marriage was all about: lineage, history, legacy. It was the bringing together of two families, not just two people. It was like the flowing together of two streams, he imagined. Everything distinct and separate in the past, but forever mingled moving forward into tomorrow.

Cassandra caught Marcus's mood and asked him for his thoughts. He demurred, still working his hardest to keep his intentions a secret. But he was so warmed internally by all he had learned of Cassandra's family during this visit that he wanted to marry her more than ever, but for deeper and deeper reasons. He wanted to connect his past with that of this family. Everything about them was interesting and different from his own, but good and strong and dignified. He liked, respected, and wanted to be a part of them. All of this came as a surprise, as he had barely even thought about, much less comprehended, what marriage actually meant from a broader familial standpoint. But now he got it, and he welcomed it like springtime after a cold winter.

Returning to the Federici home late that afternoon, Marcus and Cassandra napped on the hammock, though Marcus couldn't sleep. He gently stroked Cassandra's dark hair as she nuzzled in the crook of his neck, sleeping peacefully. He said a silent prayer that his intentions would come true, that God would bless his marriage plans and the marriage itself. He felt like a man entering the door to his future, and he wanted to step carefully, but also felt a sense of urgency. His time in Italy was drawing to an end, and his mind would not stop churning the remaining actions to be taken. He decided he'd try to get a moment alone with Giulio and see how things stood. And he had one more idea for driving home the message of Bitcoin, so when he was certain he was unobserved, he pulled out his phone and sent a text.

That evening the three Federicis and Marcus again went to a restaurant for dinner, and again there were the usual prolonged greetings and kisses. Tonight was pizza night, and it would prove to be some of the best pizza Marcus had ever eaten. At intervals of only a few minutes, the waiter arrived at the table with a pan held high, jabbering about the recipe's history and how long it had been in the family. Then he slid one piece onto each of their plates, and then another, until the pan was emptied, leaving them to eat. Moments later, almost exactly as they finished their previous helping, he arrived with another, again accompanied by enthusiastic explanations. This process continued, from red pizzas to white ones to double-deckers, with Marcus thinking each more delicious than the one before. But eventually his stomach could not accept any more appreciation from his taste buds, and he called a surrender. Cassandra and Stefania had long since left the field of battle, but Giulio ate with the appetite of two men.

As they returned home, Marcus signaled Giulio that he'd like to talk, and the two retired to the back patio once again. Crescendo scurried out the door to be with them and jumped up on Marcus's lap as soon as he was settled. Marcus had grown so accustomed to this by now that he barely noticed, scratching her behind her ears as he began to speak.

"Thanks for an amazing dinner," said Marcus. "I don't think I've ever eaten so much, and that's saying something considering how much you've fed me this trip! How do you guys not weigh 500 pounds each?"

"Ha! We're Italian! Good food is part of life! It is to be enjoyed, not rationed. But seriously, we don't snack much, because that just wastes capacity you could have to enjoy the next meal." Giulio patted his belly and sighed, clearly satisfied with the evening's intake.

"Yes, I've never enjoyed food as much as I have here. It's all so good," said Marcus.

Silence filled the space between them, as Marcus gathered his thoughts and Giulio, ever discerning, gave him the space to do so. Meantime, Crescendo licked Marcus's wrist.

"So how did it go with Ari earlier?" Marcus finally inquired.

"Ari is wonderful! You've certainly got some impressive friends, young Marcus! I think Ari knows everything there is to know about Bitcoin!"

"Did he answer your questions?"

"Oh yes. He was very informative. I'm used to this, you see, because being a Christian, a preacher, one gets accustomed to skeptics and critics. One becomes used to the same handful of objections over and over again. As I came across the pushbacks on Bitcoin online, the entire tone of that resistance felt a little like what I encounter when I share Jesus with people. Now don't get me wrong, I am not making a comparison between Jesus and Bitcoin, heaven forbid. I am just saying that in terms of believing in something and having the right information, people are quick to take negative views and entrench themselves in those views. It's what I like to call passionate ignorance. They don't know, and they don't even know that they don't know, all the while adamantly thinking they *do* know. You know? Because of this reason, and my experience as a Christian preacher, I would like to think that I am more open-minded than most. So in truth, Ari didn't have a hard job to do."

Marcus was fidgeting as Giulio said these words. This could only be a good sign, he thought. He watched Giulio carefully and chose with precision what he would say next. But before he could, Giulio spoke first.

"I know what you want to ask, and it's not time yet," said Giulio with a sterner voice than Marcus would have liked. "I want to know how one actually gets bitcoin and begins to use it? How does one invest in it? I still am totally in the dark on that part of things."

"I think for once I might be a step ahead of you," said Marcus smiling, trying to lighten the mood between them. "You see, earlier today I wondered if it might help you to speak to someone from the finance world. A professional investor. So I've got another person ready to speak with you."

"Man, young Marcus, your League of Nations Phone-a-Friend network is enormous. Where is this person from? Hong Kong? Sri Lanka? Chile?"

"Ha! Bitcoin is like that, I guess. It brings in people of all stripes from everywhere. But no, this next helper of mine is from Ohio and his name is Dan Smith. He's an investor and our biggest financial backer at our company. He actually led the seed round of investing when we were getting started."

"How do you know him?" asked Giulio.

"One of my professors at Carnegie Mellon is lifelong friends with him. When my professor heard what Ari and I were starting, he put us together. Dan has been our financial backbone ever since."

"OK, interesting. Your network impresses me, Marcus, I must tell you. It's good to have strong connections in life. Trust me, many times it's who you know that gets you through. A person who surrounds himself with ding-dongs will come out a ding-dong, but a person who makes good friends makes a good life."

"Yes," said Marcus nodding, trying to decide if that sounded more like a proverb or a fortune cookie. "Anyway, he comes from the world of investing, both venture capital and value investing, so I thought his take from a financial standpoint might be of interest to you. He's been an investor for over four decades, and he said he could be ready any time today for you to connect with him."

Giulio looked at his watch and then nodded. "I am good with now, I guess."

30

I am primarily a value investor," Dan explained once he was connected via video chat on Giulio's laptop. Marcus sat next to Giulio sharing the camera. "I analyze the fundamentals of an asset or business to determine if it's a productive place for my money. When I find something valuable, I hold it for the long-term. I don't play market timing. I'm not a trader or a speculator. I accumulate cashflow producing or appreciating assets, and snowball them over time. I put the power of compounding to work for me. That's my elevator pitch."

"Makes sense," Giulio nodded.

"So I understand Marcus has been getting you up to speed on Bitcoin, correct?" asked Dan.

"Yes. He's done a tremendous job, actually. I think I understand the why of Bitcoin, the what, some of the how it works, a bit of how it got going and gained traction, its possible future, and I have heard the arguments that rebut some of Bitcoin's critics. I guess now I am trying to learn how to get involved?"

"OK, certainly. That largely depends upon what you are wanting to do with it. I would say the best advice for a new initiate is to simply buy a little bit and start following its price action. The best way to truly learn about Bitcoin is to become a holder of it."

"OK, how do I do that?"

"Step one is to open an account with an exchange. You'll have to find one that operates in Italy, which will be easy. They work a lot like a brokerage account. Do you have one of those? Say with Fidelity, TD Ameritrade, or something similar?"

"Yes."

"OK, so you're familiar with the process. You simply go online, go through the steps to create an account, and they will collect some of your personal information and some KYC stuff."

"KYC?" asked Giulio.

"Oh, sorry, yes, it stands for 'Know Your Customer.' Here in the U.S. we have very specific rules that all financial institutions must follow in terms of collecting and verifying your driver's license, that sort of thing, and asking some rudimentary questions about your net worth, investing objectives, etc. I believe it works very similarly in Europe."

"Yes, I think it does," said Giulio.

"So that's step one. Choose an exchange, open an account, and then fund it by connecting one of your bank accounts to it and sending them some euro."

"OK, easy enough."

"Right. Then just buy a little bitcoin."

"What if I can't afford one?" asked Giulio.

"Oh. You don't have to buy a whole bitcoin. You can buy a fraction of one, all the way down to one one-hundred-millionth of a bitcoin. A denomination that small is called a Satoshi in honor of Bitcoin's creator."

"Oh, that's right, Marcus had told me that, good," said

Giulio.

"And I would possibly also recommend doing a little dollar cost-averaging, or I guess in your case, 'euro cost-averaging.' The price of bitcoin fluctuates quite a bit, and you will never be able to time the market perfectly, so it's a good approach to just set up an automatic purchase program that makes buys for you periodically. You can set the amount and the frequency right in your account with the exchange you choose. They almost all have it."

"Got it."

"The idea is that if you are convinced of the long-term outlook for Bitcoin fundamentally, then accumulating some steadily over time is a good way to participate. Insiders call it 'stacking Sats.'"

"Stacking Sats?"

"Satoshis, which are those little one-hundred millionth pieces of a bitcoin," Marcus answered.

"Oh, OK, cute."

"Yup, build a stack of them. So for long-term investors like myself, I want to accumulate as much Bitcoin as I can, and at the best prices. But I do this most effectively by buying steadily over time. Warren Buffett once said, 'The best time to buy stocks is *over time*,' and I believe that applies to Bitcoin, too. And one other thing: don't get caught up watching the daily price of bitcoin or following it too closely. Chances are if you focus on it you'll be too emotionally tied to price movements and make rash decisions about buying or selling. I've seen it happen with people. Don't be put off by Bitcoin's volatility. Remember, volatility is not risk! Lots of people get that confused, including an entire group of academic thinkers. So don't be misled. Instead, there are mental frameworks you should use when investing in a volatile asset class such as Bitcoin. When the price goes way up, just celebrate and think to yourself, 'I'm a genius,' but don't get greedy and rush to take profits. And conversely, when the price goes down, think 'Yay, Bitcoin is on sale,' and if you have the means, buy a little more. You have to move opposite of your emotions, and opposite the crowd.

"What's more, Bitcoin is paradoxical in that it is extremely unpredictable in the short-term while in the long-term it's among the most predictable. Therefore, I would say to start accumulating consistently, as I mentioned, but then don't make any conclusions about the value of your investment until at least four years later. Set it and forget it until your Bitcoin investing strategy has its fourth birthday, then take a serious look at where you stand. I predict that if you do so, your four-year assessment will be super satisfying."

"OK, that makes sense. And where do my bitcoins go when I buy them on an exchange like you say?" asked Giulio.

"Good question. If you follow what I've outlined so far, they will be held in custody by the exchange on which you bought them. That might be OK for small amounts, but the security of your bitcoins will become a higher and higher priority as you accumulate more and more. So at some point you will want to learn about wallets."

"Marcus told me a little bit about those," said Giulio.

"Yes, wallets are where you keep your private keys. Did Marcus discuss those with you?"

"Yes he did. Private keys are what I would use to access my bitcoins and send them to someone else if I wanted."

"Correct. Wallets don't actually hold your bitcoins, just the keys that access them. And there are several different kinds. Software wallets are pretty easy—they can be downloaded just like a smartphone app and are fairly secure. However, they are connected to the internet and that always presents at least a little risk. Another type of wallet is called a hardware wallet. These are devices a lot like thumb drives onto which you transfer your private keys. Once you unplug the device, your keys are stored on the device and no longer connected to the internet. Only problem is now you have to put that hardware wallet somewhere safe, as in a safe deposit box at your bank, a safe in your house, or at a private vault, something of the kind."

"What if you lose it?" asked Giulio.

"Bitcoin is what we call a *bearer asset*, meaning if you possess it, you own it. If you lose it, it's gone."

"Wow, I'll bet there's a lot of lost bitcoins then!" said Giulio.

"More than you can imagine! So when people say there will only ever be 21 million bitcoins, it's actually a much smaller supply than that. Some experts estimate that as much as 20 percent have been lost. But back to wallets, because there is one more thing I should tell you about hardware wallets. When you are first setting them up and putting your private keys on them, most of the good ones have a readout where they will give you a handful of key words. These words provide a memory seed that can be used to recover your keys even if you lose the hardware wallet."

"Really?"

"Yes. It's very important. So in some extreme cases when your country falls apart, a government tries to confiscate everything you have, a war rages through the streets, whatever, people can escape with all of their wealth in their heads as long as they have those seed words memorized."

"Oh, wait. Marcus mentioned that on the very first night we started discussing Bitcoin! It's incredible, no?"

"It totally is. There has never been a money that is so portable or so seizure resistant. Imagine when Cuba fell to Communism in the late 1950s and all of those people who had been successful in business or medicine or in universities, or whatever, were forced to flee any way they could for the shores of the United States. Many tried to bring gold coins, or gold hammered out into sheets that would fit around their legs under their pants. But most of these attempts failed, and many ended in tragedy as the wealth some were carrying made them targets for theft and murder. None of that would happen with Bitcoin. Just memorize some words and you've got your wealth in your head.

"So let's review. Step one: set up an account at an exchange. Step two: fund it by connecting it to your bank account and putting some money in. Step three: buy some bitcoin and perhaps even set up a recurring buy program. Step four: play around with different types of wallets and get good at storing and keeping control of your own private keys."

"That's it?"

"Well, the private key part can get a little complicated, although it doesn't have to be. But Marcus can show you how to do it. And you don't even have to do that step right away. You can save it for later when you get more familiar with Bitcoin. And in terms of anything else you want to do with your bitcoins, there are many options nowadays, and more and more are being developed. On the simplest level, you can use them to buy things. If someone wants to give you a product or service, and accepts bitcoin in payment, all you have to do is have their public address, usually represented by a QR code, and you can use your private keys to unlock access to your bitcoins and send some to their address."

"But I don't want to be the pizza guy," said Giulio, "so I'll probably just, what do you call it? HODL mine."

"Yes, HODL. I see Marcus really has taught you a lot. And you're right. The thing that's maybe hampering Bitcoin becoming a medium of exchange is the fact that it is appreciating in value so much. Also, here in the United States the government has classified Bitcoin as a commodity, which means that any time you spend it you have a tax event. If you had a gain, you have to declare that gain and pay your capital gain tax on it. If a loss, the same in reverse, of course. This makes for some complicated bookkeeping and a bad tax picture. So Bitcoin's 200 percent and more annual rise, paired with capital gains tax burden, means it might make more sense just to use it as a long-term investment instead of spendable money, at least for now."

"Makes sense."

"Some of these exchanges that I talked about have other features, too. They are now coming out with credit cards you can use that instead of giving you airline miles or cash back, they give you a percentage of bitcoin based on your total purchases. That's an excellent way to Stack Sats. And, this is really slick, you can actually lend your bitcoin to some of these exchanges and they'll pay you interest on them. This means that as you are HODLing for the long term, you can earn bitcoin on your bitcoin!"

"That's interesting," said Giulio.

"I think so too," answered Dan. "Many of them here in the States even allow us to deposit US dollars and keep them in there as US dollars, but get paid interest on those dollars in Bitcoin. And the interest rates are way, *way* above what banks are paying."

"All of this sounds like smart stuff to do."

"It's a whole new world. Trust me, I've been in finance for forty-three years and I've never seen the likes of what's happening now. It makes me wish I were younger!" said Dan.

"You and me both, my friend!" said Giulio.

"And finally, let's say you accumulate a nice big pile of bitcoin over time. You can deposit them at one of these exchanges and they will actually loan you fiat currency using your bitcoin as collateral. So think about it. What this allows you to do is grow your bitcoin stack over the years and never pay taxes on the gains. If you never sell, you don't pay capital gains taxes. At least that's the way it works currently in the United States. This could always change, of course. But it's a nice setup. Accumulate bitcoin, and borrow against the much-risen value of it to live your life. If Bitcoin continues to appreciate like it has in its first twelve years, you could borrow against it and pay the interest and never really worry about paying it off. The interest would seem negligible compared to the huge gains you've had from being smart enough to accumulate and hold bitcoin for the long term."

"I like it," said Giulio. "So let me ask you this, Dan. What aspects of Bitcoin do you *not* like?"

"Ah, you're very smart to ask that. Let me see . . . I think the first unfortunate part of Bitcoin is that it is difficult to explain."

"Boy, I'll say. Marcus has been working on me and also

connecting me to his smart friends, such as yourself, and I'm still not there."

"Right. Bitcoin is a little bit computer science, a little bit cryptography, a bit of game theory, requires an understanding of what money is currently and what it should be, some knowledge of investing, has quite a bit to do with economics, and even requires a little bit of geopolitical history. So that's one thing that always perplexes me: how to explain it clearly and help new people get up to speed more easily."

"And what else?"

"Second, I would say, is that it is still a little complicated to use. I told you about exchanges and wallets and the like, but getting control of your private keys and using hardware wallets is not intuitive for most people. Sending bitcoin across the network is actually easy enough, but there is no margin for error. Enter the wrong address and your bitcoins go somewhere unintended and there's no reversing it. There's no customer service hotline or company that can bail you out. So the complexity for users is a bit of a challenge, I think, although, to be fair, wallets and software interfaces have gotten and will continue to get better and better.

"And finally, I would say that it would help a lot if Bitcoin would fulfill all three functions of money. Right now it is clearly aiming for the first function, namely, being the world's best store of value. It is and can be used as the second one, a medium of exchange, but largely because of tax laws and the fact that it is currently more of a growth asset than anything else, people understandably are reticent to spend it and actually use it as money, as I said before. But don't get me wrong. Bitcoin is one of the easiest and cheapest ways to send money to anyone anywhere in the world. Even so, because of it not moving to the second function at scale yet, it therefore isn't fulfilling the third function of money, and that is as a unit of account. We don't think of things as costing X number of bitcoins yet."

"And your investment advice about it? Marcus explained to me a little of your background," said Giulio.

"My advice to people is always the same: do your own research, educate yourself, and then invest based upon fundamentals. What I mean by that is, do you see a viable use case for Bitcoin's future? Based on what it offers to the world, is it worth the risk for you to park some of the fruits of your labor into this new invention? Never, and I mean this emphatically, *never* invest in something just because someone tells you it will 'go up.' This is what is happening with nearly all, if not all, of the crappy alternative coins or alt coins out there. People get some hot tip, or hear on the news or on Reddit or from a high-profile public figure that a certain crap-coin is going 'to the moon.' With no underlying fundamentals and none of Bitcoin's characteristics, these coins are complete scams. People who buy into them because they are supposed to 'go up' are not investors. They are not even qualified to be called speculators. They are merely gamblers. As for me, I've worked too hard for my money to ever gamble with it. Gambling is a con that preys on suckers and favors the house. That's what all these other 'cryptocurrencies' are. They are hype schemes that should be completely avoided."

"Wow, you're stronger on that point than Marcus or Ari," said Giulio, looking over at Marcus who blanched a little.

"Yes, I know. I've been trying to convince those young fellas all along that there is no room for anything but Bitcoin. There is no need for others, either. Everything else is a copycat money-grabbing scam. I come from the perspective of an investor, and I've seen my share of charlatans. Bitcoin is the real deal. There's no reason to invest in anything but the best."

"Man, I'm glad to have that perspective from you. But what about the other applications some of these other coins are aiming for? Maybe doing things instead of trying to be money, for instance?"

"Anything worth doing can be built upon the Bitcoin blockchain, in what are called second level applications."

"Hmm, OK then," said Giulio, thinking. He always favored hearing multiple viewpoints on a subject, and this one fascinated him. Marcus, who had heard it all before from Dan, decided to respectfully stay quiet. Besides, it was always possible that Dan was right, he thought.

Meanwhile, although Stefania had done her best to stall Cassandra as long as she could, as she had secretly been doing for most of Marcus's visit while these sessions with Giulio were taking place, Cassandra finally slipped away from her mother and joined the men on the patio. She rolled her eyes when she saw the laptop open in her father's hands and Marcus huddled nearby.

"Let me guess," she said shaking her head.

"Busted!" Marcus smiled, reaching for her hand.

"Wanna go look at the stars?"

"How can I refuse," Marcus answered, standing up. Turning to the computer screen, he said, "Dan, I've got to go. But thank you again for your time here with Giulio. Of course you two can keep going as long as you'd like, but I've got an offer I can't refuse."

"Hi, Cassandra," said Dan loudly from the screen.

"Hello, Dan, you won't mind if I take Marcus away will you?"

"As you wish, young lady."

Cassandra and Marcus walked to the end of the street to a narrow dirt trail and clambered to the top of a small rise. It was one of Cassandra's secret places and she had not yet shown it to Marcus. In the distance the lights of Rome sparkled like gems strewn across the wide valley below, as if reflecting the stars in the black sky above. A gentle warm breeze wafted up the hill and smelled like summer, and all was completely silent.

***

Back on the patio, Giulio and Dan talked for another hour.

31

The next morning Marcus lay awake in bed. He had no idea what time it was, but the light seeping through the blinds was gray and dim, so he assumed it was quite early. His mind would not stop working through the thoughts of his next steps. The previous night under the stars with Cassandra had been magical, like all of his time here in Italy. He replayed the past days and took the measure of his progress with Giulio and their pact. He contemplated Stefania's involvement and wondered if it was good or bad. And he thought, of course, about the words he would say and the setting he would arrange for the proposal if he were given the chance.

But how to secure Giulio's formal approval? Surely with all the hours of interaction they'd had together and the help from Marcus's friends, Marcus had endeared himself to the Sicilian. He had tried to carefully read Stefania to see if she was in favor of his proposal. Mystifyingly, she was unreadable.

So he summarized his circumstances to himself as follows: Giulio understood Bitcoin exceedingly well for a beginner and there was nothing more Marcus could have possibly done on that front to have made more progress. As it was, he enlisted an economist, a journalist, and an investor, not to mention his own best efforts as a techie. Next, both Giulio and Stefania seemed to like and approve of Marcus in general, and they got along swimmingly during this trip, or so Marcus assumed. It might just be that they were super nice people and they would have treated anyone that way, he countered to himself. Or maybe this was just how Italians in general behave towards visitors. Or possibly all of the above were true. Importantly, Marcus was more in love with Cassandra than ever and knew she felt the same about him. They had only grown closer during his visit. Nonna liked him, too, which didn't count for nothing, and the most surprising fact of all, perhaps, was that even little Crescendo gave him hearty approval. If it meant winning Cassandra's hand, Marcus would love that little mutt right back.

Had he missed anything? His sleepy mind plodded back through all of this again, sifting and sorting. Then he pondered: How would he bring things to a head with Giulio? And when? It had to be soon, as the days remaining to him on this trip were few. How would he muster the courage? Friendly, smart, gregarious Giulio was approachable and fun, but certainly no pushover. What would Marcus actually say to him to inquire about the status of their agreement? And what if Giulio said no? What then? This is what made Marcus the most anxious. What would he do if he were rebuffed?

Eventually Marcus's mind tired of retracing these same concerns and allowed him to drift back to sleep. He dreamt about being in high school and late for a test but unable to find his locker. Worse, as he scurried around lost in a labyrinth of identical hallways, Marcus suddenly realized he was naked! Amazingly, nobody in school had noticed yet, so Marcus ducked into a broom closet. Inside was a giant papier-mâché salamander wearing red sunglasses, a blonde wig, and a navy New York Yankees ball cap. And it was alive. "Wake up," it said. "Marcus, wake up!" Strangely, it had Cassandra's voice. "Come on Marcus, get up now!" As if things couldn't get any stranger, the salamander began licking his face.

Marcus slid through that strange space between the dreamworld and the real one and watched the amphibian disappear and the face of Cassandra emerge in its place, the voice still imploring him to awaken.

"Morning," he smiled up at her as he came to, noticing also that Crescendo had jumped on the bed and was of course the source of the face-licking. "This is a nice surprise. You won't believe what I was just dreaming," he said, still inert on his pillow and chuckling at the fading imagery, thankful that in real life he was fully clothed.

Cassandra shook her head and interrupted. "Get up quick. It's Nonna. She's had a stroke!"

"What?" Marcus said, sitting up immediately and flinging off his covers.

"Her morning bridge club arrived and Nonna didn't come to the door. They got concerned and eventually the Carabinieri broke in and found her on the floor. She was conscious but couldn't move. Papa and Mamma have already left for the hospital. Come on, hurry!"

Marcus moved fast now, pawing through his suitcase and pulling on clothes haphazardly. In minutes they were out the door and in Cassandra's car.

"But we were with her most of the day yesterday and she seemed fine. More than fine! She walked our legs off!" Marcus protested.

"I know, I know," replied Cassandra, nodding as she leaned forward over the steering wheel as if willing the little car to go faster, grinding a gear occasionally in haste.

Marcus could think of no words to say and instead offered up a silent prayer. He prayed for Nonna's health and healing, for Cassandra and her family, and for the Holy Spirit's strength. Then he confessed his own selfishness and the thoughts he couldn't keep out of his mind. How could he think about himself and his plans at a moment like this? He asked for forgiveness and a focus on others. He asked to be strong enough to be who Cassandra needed at the moment, and he prayed to be a comfort somehow to even Giulio and Stefania.

Marcus's palms were sweaty as he reopened his eyes. His right knee was bouncing up and down reflexively. Cassandra drove as in a daze, barely aware of his presence, or of the presence of traffic signals, for that matter. The beautiful old buildings and quaint sights of the little town, everything that had seemed so fresh and inviting just days before now sped past in colorless smear. None of it meant anything just now.

***

The events of that morning proceeded like a grey fog creeping over a mountain town. Everything was obscured except what was up close. The future was only the next moment. There was no horizon and no distance. There was only now. In fact, it was one of the most *now* episodes Marcus had yet experienced in his young and privileged life. Minutes seemed to last forever and yet the day flew past. It was late evening before Marcus took note of the time, and yet he was exhausted from the day he could barely remember. How had a whole day gone by? How could he be so tired when he hadn't done anything? But when the family returned from the hospital to the Federici household late that night, saying little and dragging themselves to their rooms, Marcus collapsed into bed and was instantly asleep. Worry, he would later realize, brought its own special kind of fatigue. Helplessness brought another layer. The two in combination were exhausting.

After a fitful sleep, absent any such festivities as his crazy dream the night before, Marcus awoke early and marched to the already busy kitchen. Coffee and danishes were quickly consumed and the Federicis and Marcus drove to the hospital again, this time all in the same car. Marcus was too focused on the events at hand to notice little details like their travel arrangements. It was another day of whispers, sighs, waiting rooms, doctors speaking a language he couldn't understand, and his girlfriend crying. But Nonna was at least stable. The left side of her body was paralyzed, and the woman who loved to talk so much could now just slur her words. Only Cassandra seemed able to understand her, and only when leaning in close.

At home, Crescendo appeared confused about the sudden change in her living environment, and she instinctively picked up on the overall family heaviness. Sensing her duty, she began nuzzling Cassandra and Stefania each night when they would arrive home from the hospital, apparently abandoning Project Marcus.

As his last days disappeared in a tussle of hospital visits and worry, Marcus's prayers became more and more for the Federicis and Nonna, and less about himself and his own best-laid aspirations. He stopped taking the ring out and looking at it, knowing his plans were completely shipwrecked—at least for this voyage.

Marcus spent his final morning in Italy at the hospital. He gave Nonna a tender kiss on her right cheek, which was dry and fuzzy, and when he did so her eyes watered and she blundered a few words Cassandra strained to comprehend. Next he hugged Giulio and Stefania, each of them holding on longer and tighter than he would have anticipated. Afterward, Giulio held Marcus by each shoulder and just looked into his eyes. Saying nothing, he hugged him again. Finally he said, "Thanks for teaching me about rascal money, young Marcus. You and me, we have unfinished business," then he turned and walked away.

Rascal money, thought Marcus, *that's exactly what Bitcoin is,* at least at this stage of adoption! On the way to gaining mainstream application it must first be carried forward by those who refuse to blindly follow the herd to financial slaughter; by those with the courage to follow their convictions instead of conventions, by individuals who are passionate about freedom and justice for all people. Rascal money indeed, thought Marcus, as it dawned on him that Giulio had taught him much, even as he had tried to teach Giulio.

Forty-five minutes later Marcus and Cassandra arrived at the curb at Fiumicino airport. Cars buzzed past and people went about their business totally oblivious to the pain the two of them were feeling. Cassandra's eyes filled with tears as she attempted to hug Marcus across the front of the car with the gear shifter oddly in the way. After a moment she noticed this and ejected herself out of the driver's door and scurried around to embrace Marcus as he emerged from the passenger side. She cried openly now.

"I'm so sorry your trip had to end this way."

"No, no, come on, you shouldn't be worried about me. It's time to focus on your family and taking care of Nonna. But are you sure you don't want me to stay? I could easily extend my trip."

"You're sweet to offer, Marcus, truly. And you know I would love to have you around even if just for moral support. Well, for more than moral support. You make my soul happy, even when something like this is going on. But honestly, I know you have work to get back to and I'll be busy with Nonna, getting her into a home, managing her physical therapy, hoping we can get her back to living healthy again. It wouldn't be fair to you. So no, you go back and do what only you can do. Build your company, tend to business. I'll do what I must here with my family and then I'll be back to start school on time. It will seem long but it'll go fast. I promise. Besides, I've got a plan."

"A plan?"

"Yes." Cassandra wiped her eyes, managed a smile, then opened the back passenger door, bending over to retrieve a small, ventilated plastic crate. From inside the little grey box Marcus heard a familiar yap.

"Wait, what?" he said, wondering how he hadn't noticed this extra cargo.

"I wanted to give you something of myself. Something to keep you company through the rest of the summer. And every time you see her, you'll think of me. Besides, she isn't finished convincing you to love dogs. And don't worry, I already made all the necessary arrangements with the airline."

Marcus cackled, knowing he couldn't and wouldn't object.

He pictured himself being the guy who carries a tiny animal onto an airplane. He thought about how he had traveled all the way to Italy to 'win the girl' but would be returning with only her dog. Cassandra laughed, too, and they held each other a long time before parting. Marcus turned and toted the little grey crate through sliding glass doors that closed behind him as he glanced back at Cassandra and gave a little wave.

32

When Marcus had settled into his airplane seat, his carry-on bag secured in the compartment above and Crescendo nestled at his feet under the seat ahead of him, he took out his phone and tapped out a love message for Cassandra, sending along a photo of his new passenger licking his hand through the crate. Next he checked his text messages. The first was from Ari:

dude havent heard anything whats the news and how do things stand did giulio come through did the princess say yes to the prince inquiring minds want to know and you owe me

The next was from Katya:

I hope Cassandra's dad found our conversation helpful. The curiosity is killing me! Please keep me posted on progress of larger project (and congrats in advance)

And then Dan Smith:

I enjoyed speaking with Cassandra's father the other day. He is an impressive and quick student; I see where Cassandra gets it. I am praying for success in your undertaking and can't wait to raise a toast to the happy couple. Let me know if there is anything further I can do.

But before he could settle his mind on the best way to answer his cadre of good friends, the announcement came through the speaker that it was time to shut off electronic devices and prepare for takeoff. As the safety instruction video played too loudly and the plane taxied toward the runway, Marcus peered out the window at the land he had come to love in just a brief time. Although he could see only airport fences, he played stillshots through his mind of the sights and architecture and history he had seen. He thought about the many excellent restaurants and delectable food. He gathered from his memory the images and smells and sounds of a newly experienced land. But mostly he thought of *her*. To him, *she* was Italy. He was warmed by the abundance of new memories with and of her, but pained by the departure. A sadness welled up inside that was so strong it surprised him. Tears filled his eyes for the third time that day, and he let the feeling take over, paradoxically enjoying the ache he knew was pure.

So this is true love, he thought, and remembered the Bible verse that said, "Love is patient, love is kind—" *It also hurts,* he nearly said aloud. But he took comfort in a mysterious certainty he felt about his future with Cassandra. Mixed into the momentary hurt of separation was a deeper sense of security, of a treasure found and a future secured.

Life, like Bitcoin, he reflected, was unpredictable. It was wonderful and interesting and beautiful and sometimes hard, too. It could provide shocks, send tremors, and cut deep. But it also glistened and beckoned one into its future days, none of which were promised or guaranteed, but all of which were a gift. *Time*, he thought, *sweet time*. There can be nothing more precious. It's time with Cassandra that I'm remembering now, lost time with her that I'm grieving, and time with her in the future that I'm anticipating. Time with our good friends, with her wonderful family, and Lord willing, with our insular some-day family. Time that Nonna was running out of. Time as the rarest of commodities and the most precious of prizes. Time was the scarcest substance man would ever experience. The hardest money there ever would be. And when you find something valuable, he reflected, you do the analysis, understand the fun-damentals, buy in, and HODL! Things won't always be perfect, he thought, and life won't proceed on one unbroken trend line straight-up and to the right. But that's part of the spice of it all. You never know for sure. Experiencing it one moment at a time is the thing. Volatility and pullbacks are actually what make the ride so intense, and without it, things could never go up, or at least you wouldn't appreciate them when they did.

Just then, the passenger sitting to Marcus's right nudged his elbow and said, "Traveling on business or pleasure?"

Marcus took a moment to exit his moment of reverie, and then replied, "I guess you could say a little of both."

"What's your business?" the man asked.

"Well, what do you know about Bitcoin?"

"Not as much as I'd like. What can you tell me about it?"

la fine

AFTERWORD

I can't recall when I first heard of Bitcoin, but out of curiosity I bought a copy of *Bitcoin Magazine* from a grocery store in October of 2013, at a time when the price for one bitcoin was crossing $200. I read a few of the articles, but, with no one to blame but myself, made little sense of it. Placing the magazine on a shelf in a closet (where it still resides), I got on with my busy life and took no further notice. Then in late December of 2016, a friend mentioned Bitcoin to me and said he was consistently investing in it. Next, in April of 2017, with Bitcoin on its historic climb to its then peak of $20,000, I had my third encounter. I was in Atlanta for a charity board meeting where a friend asked me if I owned any Bitcoin. When I told him that I did not, and then asked him how one would go about doing such a thing, he told me the name of the exchange he used. Upon returning home a few days later I was stopped by the fact that the exchange wasn't open in the United States. After groping around in ignorance for a short while, I finally found one and began my journey.

I got interested in Bitcoin as an investor, and I became an investor for two reasons. First, because you can't just *save* money anymore. You must *invest* in order to have any chance of making your money last. This is because the fiat currencies we are all forced to live under are consistently being devalued. The second reason I became an investor is because whenever I entrusted my money to others, the returns were horrible to nonexistent. Conversely, each time I took control of my own money, did the research myself, and made my own moves, I prospered. There would be mistakes and losses, to be sure, but overall, my gains were many times better. This proved crucial to my entry into the world of Bitcoin because I had already taken similar steps with investing and the nature of the learning curve was therefore familiar. I had read and asked questions and took actions that educated me on money to the point where it became an enthusiasm instead of drudgery. With Bitcoin I did the same thing. The more I studied, the more I became convinced of its promise, and the deeper I dug.

Probably as a result of my enthusiasm for the topic, I frequently get asked about Bitcoin. I have found myself explaining Bitcoin time and again to people from many walks and stages of life. Often those inquiring are largely uninitiated and know little more than the buzz they hear from the news about Bitcoin 'going up' or 'being banned.' At such times I have wished for a simple book I could hand them to help follow-up on our discussion. And while there are many great books on Bitcoin available, books that I myself am deeply indebted to for my own education, somehow none of them fit the need I see with brand-new people. I am reminded of the rock group KISS, who said they simply became the band they could never seem to find to watch in concert. Many people, even if curious about Bitcoin, sadly will not read through an authoritative expository book on the subject. Let's face it, many people don't read at all. But the need to inform the curious is strong. According to a Grayscale survey of investors in 2019, of the 65 percent who didn't own Bitcoin, almost 90 percent said their lack of involvement was because they didn't know enough about it. So what I have long felt was needed was an approachable book, one that would be short, unintimidating, and maybe even fun; a book that might be read by those who otherwise likely wouldn't read anything else.

I was also inspired by my early days as an engineer in the automotive industry and a clever little book called *The Goal* by Eliyahu Goldratt. It was a fictional work that followed the life of a plant manager as he struggled to fix his professional chaos through the implementation of lean manufacturing techniques. While its subject matter might forever exclude it from the world of higher literature, it was nonetheless a clever way to teach a technical concept. And it was also memorable; here I am citing it some thirty years later.

Further, a short fictional work seeking to explain Bitcoin could also make use of some devices not available to the writer of nonfiction; to begin with, dialogue. Having two characters banter back and forth is an old trick in fictional works and dates back at least as far as Plato. Fiction would also allow for repetition, a major key to learning new concepts but something that would be clunky and disallowed in the pages of an expository book. What's more, fiction can naturally present differing points of view. Characters are not the same and shouldn't all agree. This disparity of opinions allows yet another angle for covering otherwise complicated and controversial subjects.

The result of these ideas is the book you hold in your hands. While it is indeed a work of fiction, and all its characters are strictly made up, there is one cameo appearance of note. My friend Guy Sottile, founder of the ministry *Italy for Christ*, was the original inspiration for the character of Giulio (similarities end there). Guy, it so happens, is the individual mentioned above who spoke to me about Bitcoin in 2017, and got me to finally take action. For this reason, as a tribute, I thought it fitting to base a part of this story upon his life and work. Real, too, is the Christian House and the wonderful effort it is making in the city-center of Naples, Italy. The refugee crisis depicted in this book is real, and the daily care and love the Christian House is providing for these unfortunate souls is as impactful in actual life as it was for Marcus in the fictional story. Any readers who may perhaps be moved to contribute time or resources to Italy for Christ and the work of the Christian House are heartily encouraged to do so. Contact information is provided in the pages to follow.

My goal in writing this book was to contribute to the spread of what my friend Orrin Woodward calls 'financial justice' by reaching individuals, who might otherwise not have been, with the message of Bitcoin. Whether it has succeeded in that quest, or not, is up to readers to decide.

Thank you for spending your time with me in these pages. I hope it has been educational and enjoyable. May you, along with Rascals everywhere, benefit from the amazing invention that is Bitcoin.

GLOSSARY

address: A unique identifier that corresponds to a virtual location where bitcoins can be sent

alt coins: Any alternative cryptocurrency that is not Bitcoin

Austrian economics: The school of economic theory based upon the teachings of late 19th and early 20th-century Vienna economists Carl Menger, Eugen Bohm von Bawerk, Friedrich von Wieser, Ludwig von Mises, and others. It follows long-accepted principles of classical economic thought around the idea that value is determined by individual action in free markets (see Keynesian Economics).

Bitcoin core: The original and complete implementation of the Bitcoin protocol.

Bitcoin maximalization: The theory that Bitcoin is the only cryptocurrency that is needed, and all other fall short of what Bitcoin offers.

Bitcoin winters: The periods of time when Bitcoin's price falls from previous highs and before it ascends to new heights.

binary: Mathematical term referring to a system of numbers that only has two: a one and a zero

block: An assembled list of data describing a group of transactions that happened on the network, information about all the blocks preceding it, and the proof of work the miner did to attach the block to the blockchain.

blockchain: The concatenation of the individual blocks comprising all the transactions that have so far been approved and confirmed in the Bitcoin network (see *block*); represents a public ledger of the history of all transactions.

block reward subsidy: Newly minted bitcoins received as a reward by the miner who 'wins' the 'race' to assemble the next block to the blockchain.

Byzantine Generals Problem: Allegorical name for the conundrum in computer science of needing to find trust in a system in which any individual actor(s) may not be trustworthy.

Cantillon Effect: Named after the 18th-century economist Richard Cantillon; the observation that the government and the people closest to government spending gain the most value from new money created in a fiat money system because they have access to the new money before the resulting price inflation occurs.

capital gains tax: Governmental tax on the increase in price of a property or commodity from the time it was purchased to the time it was sold and therefore 'realized.'

centralization: The concentration of power and control under a single entity, whether it be governmental, private, or technological.

cold wallet: A mechanism (possibly a printout on a piece of paper or a physical device) for storing the private keys to a bitcoin address that is disconnected from the internet. Operates under the principle that if a key is disconnected from the internet, it is not hackable.

consensus mechanism: A computer science term that refers to the process of attaining a unified agreement on the status of the network in a decentralized way.

consensus network: A network programmed to run according to a set of rules that fulfill the principles of consensus (see *consensus mechanism*).

custody: The safekeeping of something valuable.

cryptography: The field of converting ordinary plain text into unintelligible text, and vice versa; exists to store and transmit data in a protected form so that only those for whom it is intended can read and process it.

cypherpunks: Individuals who advocate for privacy and the preservation of individual freedom and identity sanctity, using strong cryptography technologies as a means toward social and political change.

decryption: Undoing an encryption to restore the original data or message so it can be read/utilized (see *encryption*).

debasement: The act of making something less valuable by dilution (see *devalued*).

decentralized: The condition of decision-making power and control being delegated away from a centralized authoritarian locus; in short, it means to *not* be controlled by a single entity (see *distributed*).

devalued: When something has its value diminished by the outside actions of a government or other entity (see also *debasement*). Occurs in the case of a fiat currency when more of that currency is introduced into circulation, thereby diminishing the value of that already in use (see *fiat money*).

distributed: Not to be confused with *decentralized*, distributed means to be spread out. In the case of the Bitcoin network, it means that the copy of the ledger (see *blockchain*) is kept and updated by all the nodes throughout the network, as opposed to one central place (see *decentralized*).

ESG investing: An acronym which stands for Environmental, Social, and Governance. This type of investing is concerned that the entity money is being put into is mindful and intentional about meeting current popular goals in those three areas.

encryption: The process of protecting information by encoding/obscuring it cryptographically so that it cannot be read or used until it is decrypted (see *decryption*).

endowment funds: Nonprofit financial institutions used to accept and invest donations from charitable contributors to the host organization; e.g. Harvard and Yale, which have two of the largest endowment funds in academia.

exchange: A business, a lot like a financial brokerage, that accepts a customer's fiat money and allows them to trade it for bitcoins (for a small fee). This is one of the most convenient ways to buy bitcoins. The process, of course, can also be done in the reverse order; bitcoins can be sold and converted back into fiat money. Most exchanges also allow the purchase of many alt coins, too (see *alt coins*).

Federal Reserve (FED): A semi-private, semi-government-controlled entity created in 1913 to serve as the central bank of the United States in every way except name; responsible for managing the overall supply of the US dollar. Its existence, operation, and 'dual mandate' of taking measures to control interest rates and unemployment are based on Keynesian Economics, which has grown increasingly controversial and is opposed by those of the Austrian Economic school (see Keynesian Economics and Austrian Economics).

fiat money: Money created by government edict or dictate without any reference to a base level of value (such as gold), and required as legal tender and payment of all taxes by the issuing government.

fractional reserve banking: The process used by commercial banks in which all but a small portion of money received on deposit is loaned out to new customers, who then often deposit those funds back in the bank, which loans them out again, keeping only a fraction in reserve each time. This cascading of debt across the economy expands the money supply tremendously (see *money supply*).

full nodes: Any computer connected to the internet that is running the Bitcoin core software program; keeps a full record of the Bitcoin blockchain and independently validates the transactions and blocks on the network.

genesis block: The very first block in the Bitcoin blockchain; produced by the software when the Bitcoin program was fist launched on January 3, 2009. All subsequent blocks in the blockchain are connected all the way back to that first block.

gold reserves: Gold bullion stored in the vaults of governments and/or their central banks.

government bond: A debt instrument that works like an "IOU" (I owe you); grants the bearer the right to a certain amount of money being paid back to them at some specified time in the future. Most bonds pay interest to the bearer twice a year during the holding period. Governments sell bonds to raise money to pay their bills.

halving: The feature in the Bitcoin core program that, approximately every four years, reduces the block reward subsidy in half (see *block reward subsidy*).

hash power: The power a computer or group of computers use to run hashing algorithms; often used to describe the total overall power being expended by all the miners operating in the Bitcoin network. The idea is that the higher the hash power, the higher the wall of protection against the Bitcoin network being hacked (see *mining* or *miners*).

hedge funds: A type of investment fund open only to sophisticated (high net worth) investors that utilizes complicated investing techniques to 'hedge' against market risk in both directions. Many hedge funds are characterized by large dollar amounts and powerful/wealthy fund managers.

HODL: Term used to describe buying and holding bitcoins for the long term. Originally a misspelling of the word 'hold', it has come to be an acronym for 'Hold On for Dear Life.'

hot wallet: A mechanism for storing the private keys to a bitcoin address that is connected to the internet (either through a computer or a mobile app); The term 'hot' is used because if it is connected to the internet, there is always the (possibly remote) chance of it being hacked (see *cold wallet*).

hyperinflation: The economic calamity in which the supply of a fiat money is inflated so much that its value is destroyed; this risk is inherent in all fiat currencies and has happened many times throughout history, leading to massive suffering among the affected populace.

immutable scarcity: The particular feature of Bitcoin that its predetermined supply cannot in any way be manipulated, thereby ensuring its ongoing scarcity and value.

inflation: There are two types to consider: the first is called monetary inflation, which is the condition resulting from a central bank or government increasing the amount of its currency in circulation. The second is called price inflation, and it almost always follows (and is caused by) monetary inflation. Price inflation is the increase in prices resulting from an increase in the money supply.

Keynesian Economics: A school of economic thought, popular today with governments and central banks around the world, based upon the teaching of early 20th-century economist John Maynard Keynes. Its central tenet is that deficit spending leads to economic growth, and that centralized control of a fiat money supply is the optimum and necessary method to be used to control an economy.

ledger: A record of transactions; as applied to Bitcoin, the blockchain being built by the running of the Bitcoin program is a public ledger of all the confirmed transactions that have ever taken place in the Bitcoin network.

medium of exchange: One of the three main functions of money (see also *store of value* and *unit of account*). It means that the item in question, though it often and even needs be has no other useful function, can be used in exchange for a desired good which has a specific function.

miners (mining): Computers running the Bitcoin core program involved in gathering a set of transactions found on the Bitcoin network, assembling them into blocks, and through the proof of work exercise, seeking to have them 'written' onto the official Bitcoin blockchain (see also *blocks*, *blockchain*, and *proof of work*).

monetary policy: As concerns the Bitcoin protocol, it refers to the preprogrammed and unchangeable plan for how new bitcoins get 'minted' into the network, how many, and at what rate. This is one of the key features of Bitcoin, because it is pre-known and locked, and therefore a dependable store of value. Whereas fiat currencies have monetary policies controlled by central banks largely behind closed doors, and the amount and rate of new money issuance has no limits.

money supply: General term used to refer to the amount of a fiat currency in circulation in all forms (coins, paper, digital, etc.).

Nakamoto consensus: The name given to Bitcoin's decentralized protocol which is considered Bitcoin's main innovation and key to its success; involves many features to accomplish the operation of a trustless system that doesn't require any 'trusted' third parties, and yet can withstand attack from bad actors.

node: Computer connected to the Bitcoin network by running the Bitcoin Core software program (see *Bitcoin core*).

number-go-up technology: The somewhat whimsical term applied to the Bitcoin protocol because of its increasing price performance, over time, thanks to its unchangeable and pre-known monetary policy (see *monetary policy*).

peer-to-peer: The condition wherein two parties, unknown to each other, can interact directly without a 'trusted' third party such as a bank or other type of central intermediary.

permissionless: The characteristic of the Bitcoin protocol that allows anyone to transact, at any time, and from any place, without having to first secure the approval of a third party.

price action: The movement of the price of something in the free market.

private key: A secret number used to unlock and access one's bitcoins on the Bitcoin network (see *public key* and *public/private key pair*).

proof of work: The algorithm used by miners to confirm transactions on the Bitcoin network and to 'write' new blocks onto the blockchain (see miners, block, and blockchain).

public key: A public number used to receive and lock bitcoins on the Bitcoin network (see *private key* and *public/private key pair*).

public/private key pair: The combination of a private unlocking key and a public locking key used to transact with one's bitcoins on the Bitcoin network.

renewable energy: Refers to sources of energy generation that do not rely on the consumption of fossil fuels.

sovereign wealth funds: Professionally managed investment funds consisting of the wealth of a nation-state and/or ruling family.

stock-to-flow ratio: Economics term describing the total amount of a good available in storage versus the new amount that can be mined/obtained in a year; the higher the stock-to-flow ratio, the less the overall supply of the good changes (meaning, the less its total supply responds to an increase in demand) and the better it is as a store of value (see *store of value*).

store of value: One of the three main functions of money (see also Medium of Exchange and Unit of Account); the ability of a money to maintain its value through time.

Sybil attack: Named after the subject of the book *Sybil* (the case study of a woman with dissociative identity disorder), refers to an attack on a system by creating a large number of pseudonymous identities to gain a disproportionately large influence.

transaction: The moving of any amount or fraction of bitcoins on the Bitcoin network

treasury: The government entity in charge of the wealth and money of a nation; usually responsible for the collecting of taxes, holding of reserves, issuance of debt, and paying of bills.

trustless: A system in which no parties have to rely on the integrity of the other parties involved. Instead, the protocols of the system ensure the integrity of any and all interactions.

unforgeable costliness: As applied to Bitcoin, means that the work done by miners costs something real in actual terms, which is a barrier to entry that prohibits easy counterfeit participation by bad actors (see *miners*).

unit of account: One of the three main functions of money (see also *medium of exchange* and *store of value*) that refers to the pricing of goods in that money system. This would be true of Bitcoin if goods and services were to be priced in bitcoins, as in, 'That home is for sale for 10 bitcoins.'

wallet: Any type of device (either software, hardware, or even paper) that stores the private keys to a Bitcoin address (see *private key*).

For donations, inquiries, and support:

Italy for Christ (and the Christian House)
1301 Shiloh Road NW, Suite 321
Kennesaw, GA, 30144

Italyforchrist.it

ACKNOWLEDGEMENTS

The creation of a book often begins as a solitary event—a ship captained by a lone soul. Soon, however, the boat fills with crew, responding to a distress signal, who strive mightily to sail the weary vessel as the bewildered captain realizes the voyage would have floundered were it not for the assistance of so many. I would like to thank the crew so crucial to this voyage. Without them, we would never have made port.

Thanks first and always to my wife Terri, who as a writer herself is consistently both my best critic and encourager, and who provided much insight into what might be necessary to teach someone unfamiliar with Bitcoin. Thanks also to my long-time business partner Orrin Woodward and his wife Laurie for careful readings, great feedback, and undying support. Endless gratitude is also due my lifelong friend Rob Hallstrand for tireless exertions on my behalf. Thanks to Steve Kendall for ensuring the quality of the finished product, and to Jordan Woodward for the graphics and building of the book. You two are consummate professionals and a pleasure to work with. Special thanks to my seventeen-year-old daughter Christine Brady (who requested her royalties in Bitcoin) for a marvelous job designing the cover and capturing my vision with the exact right look. Thank you, Steener, for also giving a careful reading of the manuscript and teaching me much about writing. Thank you also to Martin Spusta for dedication, energy, friendship, and sheer commitment to excellence, and to Eyad Kassem (AKA 'Q') for technical assistance and fact checking of the manuscript. Thanks to my parents, brother, and children for your love, encouragement, and support. I am beyond blessed to have you as family. Thanks also to Doug Huber for running all the little things in my life and keeping me from being overwhelmed. Thanks to Doug Bookman for your friendship, teaching, and always being willing to listen to more about Bitcoin. I also want to thank Art Jonak for being a great source of information and insight into many topics. Thanks also to Chris Swanson for always being willing to serve. Special thanks to everyone associated with Life, both at the corporate offices and in the field; it is an honor to work with such Rascals.

Thanks especially to Guy and Sondra Sottile for allowing me to use a bit of their life and work as the backdrop for this story. Also thank you to everyone associated with *Italy for Christ*, particularly its extraordinary board members David Sawkins, Bob Higgins, Craig Wendel, Kenny Foreman, Byron Attridge, Brock Hattox, Ralph Nicosia, and William Boerop. Also thanks to Betsy Plunkett for keeping us all straight. Gratitude goes out to the 'Tribe' in Italy, including Alessandro Iovino, Davide Lepore, Giovanni Tagliaferri, Marco Palma, and everyone associated with *The Christian House*; may God continue to prosper your good works to His glory. I hope that my depiction of your efforts is edifying and worthy.

I would also like to express heartfelt gratitude to all the podcasters and writers in the Bitcoin space; you have provided a fascinating education for which I am grateful. May you continue to inspire and inform others as you have me.

Also, a salute to Satoshi Nakamoto and all the Bitcoin developers who have worked to bring decentralized money into the world. May your invention continue to take flight into the skies of financial freedom and justice for all.

Finally and above all, I give honor and glory to my Lord and Savior Jesus Christ. May all who read these pages come to know Him better.

If I messed anything up in these pages, which is highly likely, the fault lies only with me. We can laugh about it together.

ABOUT THE AUTHOR

Chris Brady is a #1 *New York Times* bestselling author and the CEO of Life, LLLP. He and his wife Terri have four children and one grandson and live in North Carolina.

chrisbrady.com